Building Leaders Through Service®

The Qualities of Serving Leaders

STUDENT EDITION

Always keep serving!

Dave Kelly

Dave Kelly

America's Student Leadership Trainer^sm

The International Student Leadership Trainer^sm

Professional Speaker, Trainer, Author, and Coach

Thank you and Dedication

As you read this book, you will see that there have been a lot of people who influenced me along my journey as a visionary serving leader. Advisors, teachers, friends, family, fellow students, and more. I cannot possibly name everyone who has been a part of me becoming the kind of leader and speaker that I am. There are a few, however, who have helped me to get to where I am today with the program that inspired this book.

There are college student life coordinators who encouraged me to follow my love of community service and share how my leadership skills, thoughts, and abilities are rooted in those experiences:

Jeff Foote from SUNY-Cobleskill was the first school staff member to recognize and ask me to share my commitment to service with his students and then suggested I offer it to other campuses.

Tom Faessel from the University of Akron believed in this program when very few others did. He knew that this topic provided a special spark for me and brought it to his campus.

Sharinda Welton from the University of Findlay has served alongside me at numerous events and shared with me her love for serving others. I will never forget her helping me push a cart loaded with about 20 crates of peanut butter and jelly sandwiches, clothing, toiletries, and other donations to a shelter for the hungry and homeless seven blocks away through the sweltering streets of New York City's Hell's Kitchen in July – all while wearing heels and a nice business suit and then going straight to a luncheon without having the opportunity to change. I thank all of them and the many other coordinators who have supported my mission to leave a legacy of service with students everywhere. You are making this a better world for all we serve.

I am so appreciative to all the students with whom I have interacted on my journey as a volunteer, advisor, and speaker. You are the reason I do what I do and I thank you for allowing me to be a part of your lives.

My Kiwanis Family has also played an important part in my growth as a serving leader. I have been blessed to know many dedicated Kiwanis members who not only work and live in their communities but serve in them as well. My fellow Circle K District Administrators were always very generous in their support and shared ideas that helped make our organization in Georgia better. In turn, they allowed me to share our success stories with them.

Georgia Circle K will always be important to me as it shaped who I am as a leader, advisor, and speaker. Special thanks to the nine Governors I served with who had a huge impact on me and allowed me to have an impact on them when I was District Administrator: Julie, JenGayle, Carol, Rebecca, Devin, John, Patsy, Katie, and Blaire. I also thank all the students and advisors with whom I was privileged to work with throughout the state of Georgia.

Throughout my speaking and training career, the staff and members of the Association for the Promotion of Campus Activities (APCA) have generated incredible love and support to me and my vision to serve the students of our world. I am thankful all of them, especially the founder and Executive Director of APCA Eric Lambert and his awesome wife, APCA Vice-President Heather Lambert. They have provided many opportunities for me to work with students and truly have servant hearts when it comes to our member schools, associates, and students. Their support and promotion of the *APCA Serves!* program, which I lead, has opened the door of service to thousands of students who might not otherwise have gotten involved and engaged. I am grateful to everyone involved with APCA who has allowed me to have this career that I love so much.

My family has been committed to service and serving others throughout our lives. I will talk about my daughters more in the body of the book, but I am so proud of them both and thank them for being serving leaders who make a difference at home and in the world. I love you both very much, Amanda and Katie, and I appreciate you supporting my career as a speaker and author.

This book and my speaking career literally would not be possible without the love, support, encouragement, pushing, and belief in me that my wife Dia Stokes Kelly has given me. She was there when I was trying to figure out how to get going as a speaker. She is the one who suggested I focus on students as my speaking and training niche. She refused to let me give up on myself during some of the low times, actually threatening me if I gave up on my dream. She is the editor of my books, blogs, newsletters, presentations, and my most vocal critic and fan. All that I am in this world is because of her, the love of my life.

I am only able to bring this book to you because of the talents and abilities endowed in me by my Creator, the Lord God. I thank Him, Jesus, and the Holy Spirit for all They have given me and the doors They continue to open for my career.

Finally, this book is dedicated to you. I hope you enjoy reading about my journey into leadership and my thoughts on the qualities of visionary serving leaders. Please make these qualities a part of who you are and your daily life. The world needs you and you can make a difference in it. Thank you!

Other Books by Dave Kelly

Building Leaders Through Service: The Qualities of Visionary Leaders [Community Leader Edition]

Gonzo's Little Book of Motivation (Second Edition)

The Sermon on the Mount: The Greatest Motivational Speech Ever

All are available directly from the author by going to https://bit.ly/3pC15nh or ordering from Amazon.com

Introduction

I have been a lover and believer of service since I was very young. When I was a kid, the Keep America Beautiful campaign (www.kab.org) released a public service announcement which became known as "The Crying Indian" in 1971. The ad showed a Native American paddling through a litter-strewn river, surrounded by smog and pollution. As he gets out of his canoe on a plastic waste-infested shore by a freeway, a car passes him and tosses a bag of garbage at his feet. This causes him to turn to the camera with a single tear from his right eye rolling down his cheek, signifying his despair at what has become of a land that once was so beautiful. (You can view the ad at https://bit.ly/3O10eqk.)

That image stuck with me, and it motivated me to want to pick up litter, to do my part to keep the environment clean. That grew into a larger desire to serve others and I continued to serve throughout high school, college, and into my adult life. I met my wife because of our love of community service. Both of my daughters have been and are engaged in different ways with service opportunities. It is who we are.

As a professional speaker, I focus largely on community service and civic engagement, with several programs designed to engage students in serving others. This style of leadership is best known as servant leadership. Yet, I have had students who told me they do not like the term because it implies the person who is serving is in some sort of involuntary servitude.

In searching for a different term to use, I decided on "serving leader" to be more descriptive of how I think this works in practice:

Servitude is an involuntary obligation or forced indenture. Servant Leadership is a positive attitude and/or approach. Serving Leadership is putting that attitude into action.

When you are in **servitude**, you are forced to be someone's servant to do as they dictate, without choice, and possibly without compensation, for your efforts.

Servant leadership is how you approach service opportunities, making a conscious decision to serve with a joyful heart, for the good of the group, or for an agreed upon reward or compensation.

Serving leadership is taking the positive attitude of a servant leader and bringing it to your work, your service, your leadership, etc. It is not drudgery, it's fun!

In this book, I share qualities that I believe serving leaders embody and I illustrate those characteristics with a variety of stories. In the end, I will ask you to make a service commitment and share it with me, and the world, at www.facebook.com/BuildingLeadersThroughService.

But, first, more about my journey into leadership.

Chapter One

My Journey into Leadership

My journey into leadership began when I was 16 years old. In high school, I was a member of Key Club (a community service organization sponsored by Kiwanis International) in North Fond du Lac, Wisconsin. I was not an officer, nor did I hold any sort of leadership role, I was just a very active member. I joined the club because the band director, Mr. Johnson, was the faculty advisor. I decided if he thought Key Club was cool enough to be the advisor, then I would join it because I was in band, jazz band, chorus, swing choir, and the school musical. As you can see, I hung out with him a lot!

Near the end of my junior year, our club president told us about a convention going on in Green Bay. My high school was in a small village of about 4,000 people. At the time, Green Bay had about 80,000 people and I was excited about going to the big city for the weekend. I worked the summer before on a dairy farm and had saved some money to take a girl to prom. But when I asked her to go with me, she turned me down. She was waiting for this other guy to ask her.

And he never did! HA!

So, I got to go to Green Bay and she had to stay home!

Well, when I got to Green Bay, I was totally blown away. There were over 600 hundred high school students there. Our high school only had a total of 400 students! Moreover, students were running the sessions. They had adult advisors, but as far as emceeing and talking during the sessions, it was all student led.

The first night, we all had to go to caucuses to listen to the campaign pitches of students running for the (Wisconsin & Upper Michigan) district board. There were three executive level positions that everyone would vote on and then each division (a portion of the district) would also elect a representative during the caucus meetings. There were two divisions in our room: ours was Division 3, comprised of seven or eight clubs from east central Wisconsin; and Division 8, comprised of nine or 10 clubs from north central Wisconsin.

As we sat in our caucus, students running for the executive positions came in to talk to us. They had literature and platforms and told us what they would do if we would elect them. In between these candidates, a guy would get up in front of the students representing Division 8 and tell them what he would do if they would elect him to be their representative, also known as Lt. Governor.

"Hmmm, ok," I thought.

As this went on, the student serving as District Secretary was up front begging someone from our side of the room to run for Division 3 Lt. Governor. Apparently, no one had served in that capacity for several years and they really wanted someone to fill the position. Despite a lot of asking and cajoling, no one stepped forward. Finally, my advisor nudged me and said, "Why don't you do it?"

My response was, "Me? How can I do that? I have never even been an officer in our club. I don't know what that Lt. Governor thing is. How can I be on the district board?"

But I thought about it. I realized that I could raise my hand and say, "I'll do it." Once I got in front of everybody, they would see that I was not any good and didn't know anything, then someone better could be elected.

So, I raised my hand and said, "I'll do it."

And, I learned a lesson about volunteering that night.

I learned that you tend to get what you volunteer for... because no one ran against me.

I got up in front of the group in my dad's suit coat and my clip-on tie. I answered their questions the best I could. I guess I wasn't a total loser because they elected me — they really didn't have any choice! And that was my first foray into a student leadership position.

Leaders take risks

I took the challenge. I dove into the great unknown of leadership. It was exhilarating and scary at the same time. So, what to do next?

I came home from that convention and dove into all the material I was given, and I did everything that the books and manuals told me to do. I had a successful year and, at the convention at the end of our term, two of the Lt. Governors in our district (out of 14) were named as "Outstanding".

I was one of them.

Then, the powers that be of our district had to choose one us to be the nominee for the Key Club International Outstanding Lt. Governor award.

They picked me.

That summer, in Washington, DC, at the international convention, in front of 3,000 people, out of over 700 Lt.

Governors in the whole organization, only 14 were named as outstanding.

I was one of them.

I was not able to be there to accept the award due to an emergency appendectomy a few days before the trip. But I was very excited and extremely proud, nonetheless.

And a bit disappointed. All of this happened for me during my senior year of high school. I had a great time serving on the district board, getting to be a leader, visiting other high schools with clubs, and planning service projects.

And then, it was all over.

I thought to myself, "Wow, I wish I had known about all of this sooner. I could have been a Lt. Governor earlier and then maybe even have served in one of the executive positions in the district or even on the international board." But no. It was all over for me.

Or so I thought.

At our Key Club district convention, I had met a guy named Mike who was the District Governor for Circle K International (now commonly known as "CKI"), the collegiate level of Key Club. I told him I was going to the University of Wisconsin-Oshkosh. He shared with me that there was a Circle K chapter at that school, but it was inactive.

We talked about me getting the chapter reactivated and then he would help me move up the CKI ladder. A fellow Key Club Lt. Governor was also going to school there, so we decided that we would rebuild the chapter together that fall with me serving as the president and he as vice-president.

This would set me up to run for District Governor that spring, with Mike preparing me for the job. After a year serving on the district board, I would seek a spot on the international board. Since there were nine vice-president positions, elected at-large, I would go for that first, and then I would run for international president prior to my senior year.

It was a perfect plan.

Then fate stepped in.

I had plans to go to the international convention in Chicago that summer, to get to know the Circle Kers in attendance from our district, particularly the district board members.

About a week before the international convention, Mike called to inform me that the Lt. Governor of our division was not going to be able to return to school that fall and thus was resigning his position.

Mike asked me if I wanted the job.

I let a pregnant pause go by for effect. Then I said "yes," wrung my hands and emitted an evil laugh!

This development played into my plans perfectly. I would be better poised to run for Governor as a freshman if I was already serving on the district board. Everyone knew what Mike was up to and no one was willing to stand in my way. I did reactivate my club – with my friend as president – and another club at a nearby school. I used my Key Club contacts to recruit members and did the best job I could. I was a shoo-in, since no one would dare run against me.

Until…

I heard rumblings that our District Secretary-Treasurer, Dianne, was also considering running for Governor.

Everyone loved Dianne. She was awesome. Barely five feet tall and a bundle of energy and enthusiasm for Circle K. She had served as District Convention Chair the previous year and was doing an amazing job in her current role. If she ran against me, I would be toast.

At least, that was the conventional wisdom.

I never thought that. I was determined to make my way to the top of Circle K International and I was not going to let anyone get in my way. I had written "I am Circle K International President" over and over in a notebook and would do so until I ran for the position. (That was my first exposure, even though I did not know it at the time, to the power of affirmations.)

Dianne and I talked in January at our pre-convention board meeting. The convention, and the election, would be the first weekend in March. She told me she thought I would be a great Governor and would not run against me. I breathed a sigh of relief, but I knew that others were not sure about me and they were still working on Dianne.

I announced my candidacy the first week of February by sending letters (individually written on my old, manual typewriter) to all the club presidents in the Wisconsin-Upper Michigan District, as well as to the district board members. I was committed to running for Governor. Nothing was heard from Dianne or anyone else for that matter. Step two of my plan seemed to be well in hand.

Until…

I got to the convention hotel, in my college hometown of Oshkosh. I saw Dianne and I gave her a big hug. And as I stepped back, she held her arms around my waist and told me she was going to run for Governor.

#@&%

That was what I thought, for a moment, anyway. But, in the next moment I decided, "Bring it on. I will run the best campaign I can. I will share my vision for the district and I will show everyone that I am most qualified to serve as District Governor."

Leaders do not back down in the face of obstacles

I looked back down at Dianne and said, "Well, welcome to the race. May the best person win." And with a big smile she told me, "I'm just kidding!"

Ever since that day, I have hated the phrase, "I'm just kidding!" Or, today's shorthand, "JK!"

She gave me a big hug and again told me how she thought I would be a great Governor and she was totally supportive of me.

The rest of the convention was more of a coronation than an election, although I did have to answer questions about running unopposed.

"I think there are a lot of qualified people who could be seeking this position, but I have been openly supported by them and I think they share my vision for the district." And many of those people ultimately served in positions on my board.

We had a great year. We thought outside of the box before anyone even knew what that meant. We set several records including number of new chapters started (we use the terms chapter and club interchangeably), membership growth, and community service.

At the end of the year, we held our district convention in LaCrosse, Wisconsin, literally in the middle of the Mississippi River. Our attendance was record setting and during the House of Delegates session (where elections and changes to the bylaws took place), I delivered the "State of the District Address" and compared our year to the original "Rocky" movie. This was right after the first sequel came out and Rocky had won the heavyweight boxing title. I compared our year to the movies, of the ascension of Rocky against overwhelming odds, turning defeat into victory, and challenging the status quo. I got a standing ovation.

And that night, I got something better. Validation.

We had a dance party with a DJ and some of my board members got the DJ to play the theme to "Rocky," a song by Bill Conti called "Gonna Fly Now." They came over, put me up on their shoulders, and carried me around the dance floor. Wow! I raised my arms in victory, like a boxer in the ring. It was one of the best nights of my life.

I gave my farewell address the next day, with few dry eyes in the house. Then I set my sights on the next part of my plan: Circle K International Vice-President.

The election was to be held at the Circle K International Convention in Philadelphia that summer. I worked on receiving endorsements from our district and surrounding ones, such as Michigan and Indiana. I felt pretty good about my chances since there were nine spots to be elected.

However, I did not want to appear over-confident, so I worked as hard as I could. Out of nearly 500 ballots cast, I was the only one of the nine elected with 100% of the vote. That seemed to bode well for my run the following year for International President. Some people even asked me why I was not running for International President at that convention. I told them I had time and wanted to have the experience of serving districts outside of my own as a Vice-President.

The real reason was that I had expected Mike to be running for International President. He had served as International Vice-President during the term that was ending. Everyone thought he would throw his hat into the ring, but he didn't. However, he was still committed to helping me get to the ultimate prize.

But, first things first. I believe in doing a good job in the position you currently hold before you seek another one. I threw myself into my vice-president role, working with three districts and serving on international committees. I was recognized as a top candidate for president and ran for the position at our international convention in Ft. Worth, Texas, against three other vice-presidents, all of whom I considered to be good friends of mine.

I knew it was going to be a tough battle, so I sought the advice of some of the past international presidents. One of them told me, "Get your supporters, but be everyone else's second choice." So, that was how I approached the campaign. Work hard in my strong-holds but work harder in those of my opponents.

The good news: I got through the first round. The bad news: out of 430 delegates, my opponent only missed winning on the first ballot by 25 votes. I was way behind, in second place.

My opponent was the first truly legitimate and viable female candidate in the organization's history as we had only opened membership to women just nine years earlier. There was a lot of sentiment that it was time for a woman president. What could I do?

Leaders step up in the face of adversity

I worked as hard as I could, campaigning deep into the night. I solicited and received the support of the two candidates who had been eliminated. But would their supporters follow them?

The election was held on Wednesday morning of the convention. Had it been any earlier, I don't think I would have had a chance. I received a key endorsement around 3:30 am that day.

My opponent, Cecilia, and I were seated next to each other at the head table. We gave our final speeches. The ballots were marked and taken up. I turned to Cecilia and said, "Well it's over. We don't know who has won yet, but we can collapse now." The rest of the business was a blur while we waited for the result.

Finally, the elections committee re-entered the room. Someone had won. Cecilia and I perked up. We finished the business on the floor and then waited for the chair of the elections committee to come forward and announce the result.

In fashion typical of this type of thing, he did his best to draw it out.

He announced, "Ladies and Gentlemen, you have elected a new Circle K International President. Your new president is a past District Governor…"

…which we both were.

"A current international vice-president…"

…which we both were.

A student at the "University of…" (long pause)

…which both of our schools started with. But hers was Boca Raton and mine was Wisconsin-Oshkosh.

After the longest of pauses he continued.

"Wis…"

Which was all my supporters needed to hear. Half the room exploded immediately into applause and cheers. The other half of the room joined in, moments later, after their "what just happened" shock. Cecilia and I hugged, and I stepped up to give my remarks as the president-elect.

I was inducted into office later that day and had an awesome time as president. I got to travel all over the world to some really cool places: Vienna, Austria; the Bahamas; Canada; Los Angeles, California; New York City; and even Aberdeen, South Dakota, in February. [Ok, some places were more cold than cool.]

I learned so much about student leadership and working with people in leadership roles. I also learned a lot about interacting with professional staff people assigned to work with students. This latter experience would help me in future roles as an advisor and mentor.

I also found that I loved speaking in front of audiences, giving speeches, and presenting workshops. For a theatre major, it was the best thing ever! That led me to think about a career as a professional speaker. More on that later, though.

My journey into leadership was far from over. It continued a little closer to home.

After an awesome year as international president, I settled into my final year of school to focus my attention on my campus leadership roles and on graduating. You see, even while all the above was going on, I was also a leader on my campus. I served one year as the Theatre student representative in the lower house of our student government, called the Assembly, which led me into greater involvement with the Oshkosh Student Association (OSA).

After representing the Theatre area, I was elected as a Student Senator from the College of Letters and Science. I served three terms in the Senate and became well-known on campus as an SGA leader. During the year that I was serving as Circle K International President, I ran for an SGA executive office. At UW-Oshkosh, the President and Vice-President candidates ran as a slate. A fellow Senator named Robin wanted to run with me. It was her idea for me to be on the top of the ticket as President and she would run for Vice-President, meaning that she would work with the Student Senate.

There was a problem, though. The OSA Constitution stipulated that neither the President nor Vice-President could be an executive officer of another organization **on** campus. I was serving as Circle K International President, which I did not want to give up. I thought I was safe because, technically, I was not an executive officer of a club **on** campus. The Dean of Students, who was the SGA advisor, along with the reigning president and vice-president did not see it that way, mainly, I contend, because they were supportive of our opponents.

What to do? I had to lose the election or at least deflect some attention should we win.

So, I took the #2 spot on the ticket and promoted Robin to #1. She was a great Senator and would be a wonderful president if we won. Besides, the real power of OSA was in the Senate, so if I did win VP, that's where I wanted to be. However, I knew a lot of people would not support a ticket with me in the #2 slot, only #1. But I rolled the dice.

I was traveling a lot then, going to district conventions every weekend, so much so that the onus for campaigning was on Robin. She worked very hard and I did what I could. We were promised the endorsement of the student newspaper by none other than the editor himself, yet when the *Advance-Titan* came out the week before the election, our main opponents were endorsed, with the editorial concluding that a flipping of our ticket may have changed their minds.

Rats!

We lost. My first ever (and still only) election defeat. But I was okay. I still was the President of Circle K International and I had really elevated my stature. In fact, the new president asked me to become the Legislative Affairs Director for OSA which meant that I would be our chief lobbyist and liaison to the United Council of University of Wisconsin System Student Governments (UC, for short). I also asked to be appointed as the Chair of the Committee on Committees.

Huh?

Yeah, the Committee on Committees could be very powerful. Wisconsin has a statute that requires shared governance at University of Wisconsin system institutions. This meant that any university committee has to have an equal number of students and faculty and administration on the committee. Well, for a number of years, this committee was left dormant and the Senate always scrambled to get enough students to serve on committees, meaning that most of the time the faculty and administration could do what they wanted.

Not on my watch!

Leaders take responsibility

I took this responsibility very seriously and committed myself to filling every committee slot available to students. The first step I took was to enforce the Senate rule that all Senators must serve on at least two university committees — or lose their seat! This rule gave me great leverage. I had the ability to appoint Senators to the good committees or the less desirable ones and they had to serve regardless. I feel that serving leadership is the best model for any leader, so I decided that every committee that had the voice of students represented was a good one! I asked the Senators to give me their preferences and I worked to put them where they would be most happy.

This further elevated my profile and I was elected by my fellow Senators as the Vice-President Pro-Tempore of the Senate, effectively the number three person in student government. I began to assume a leadership role unprecedented in the Oshkosh Student Association: I was Vice-President Pro-Tempore of the Senate; a member of the Executive Board; Legislative Affairs Director; a member of the Executive Staff; and Chair of the Committee on Committees, which also meant all requests for committee appointments (even by the president) came through me.

I used these opportunities to get more students involved in

student government, to push initiatives that I wanted to have happen, and change the power dynamic in OSA. I essentially usurped the Vice-President in importance as everyone looked to me for direction. The President consulted with me and confided in me more than his elected #2!

How cool, even though I lost the previous election.

Shortly after January 1, the Director of Legislative Affairs for UC resigned. I applied for the job, a paid position, and was hired. I had to resign my OSA positions to take on this new leadership role. But I was willing to do it because it was so cool!

I got to work in Madison, the state capital. I met with state legislators every day. For a political science major (yup, I majored in that, too), this was nirvana. I had a schedule that allowed me to commute from Oshkosh (about 90 miles) and still take care of my duties. It was an amazing sequence of events that led me to this point, but it was a willingness to take risks that opened doors for me.

I even had one of our Senators come and spend a day with me to see what my job was like. I later endorsed him and his running mate for president and vice-president, over my successor as VP-Pro-Tempore and the Vice-President that I had usurped. My guys won! And they did such a great job, that OSA received the Chancellor's Award from the Board of Regents as the best UW student government in the system. Can I see talent or what?

Of course, all good things must come to an end. For me, that was my college graduation. I became the first member of my family to graduate from college, with a Bachelor of Science Degree in Speech and Political Science. I graduated with honors and was named as an Outstanding Senior by UW-

Oshkosh and included in <u>Who's Who Among Students in American Colleges and Universities</u>. I was even mentioned by our graduating class speaker for having served as Circle K International President!

So, where would this journey of leadership take me next?

Leaders look for opportunities to serve

After a couple of years of focusing on getting my career started, I decided to return to my community service roots. I had been hanging around Circle K as an alumnus, so I took the plunge and dove into Kiwanis. By this time, I had moved to Atlanta, so I joined a club there and started moving up the leadership ladder.

Near the end of my first year of membership, the Georgia Circle K District Administrator, George "Dad" Gray, invited me to become a member of his team as an Assistant Administrator to work with Circle K clubs throughout the state. I was going to be able to take what I had learned as a member, teach it to a wide range of clubs, and hopefully impact hundreds of students.

I got fully involved in the organization by helping at club membership recruitment drives, attending club and district meetings, mediating disputes, overseeing conferences and conventions, and more. I developed a very strong bond with our district board members, as well as many members throughout the state. I discovered that I had a real talent for working with students and helping them develop their leadership skills.

I served in the assistant role for nine years (four with "Dad" and five with his successor, Ron Jackson) and then I was appointed District Administrator in 1998. When I took over as administrator, we had eight active chapters in good standing with Circle K International, with 222 dues paid members. Because I had several years to plan my approach to this position, I was able to study how other administrators lead their districts. Many of my colleagues were fully hands off, with a philosophy of letting the students do what they wanted. Others were a bit overbearing, getting into the minutiae of every activity and project.

Due to the unique nature of the overall Kiwanis/Circle K relationship, I saw this role as a partnership with the students, where they could run their organization in an environment that encouraged trying new things, while still providing a safety net that would keep them from getting hurt. They would develop their leadership skills by serving, but also through their connection to my administrative team.

By the time I retired as District Administrator, nine years later, we had 593 members in 28 clubs in good standing. Thirty-four of our students had received Distinguished District Officer recognitions from Circle K International; Georgia had received seven Distinguished District Awards; and I had been named as a Distinguished District Administrator for each of my nine years, the most ever in the organization's history. And my nine straight awards are also a record.

Since retiring as District Administrator, I have taken my show on the road, sharing my knowledge of student leadership and campus organizations at colleges and universities across the country. I have also presented professionally more than 600 times, for more than 300 different colleges and universities, many of whom are repeat customers, and I look forward to many more in the years to come. I present in-person, virtually, and in hybrid environments.

That is my journey to this point. I will share more stories in the pages and chapters to come. Let's get started on your journey as a Serving Leader!

Discussion/Reflection Questions

1. Think about your journey into leadership: How has it impacted upon the person you are today?

2. What is a risk you have taken in leadership?

3. When are times that you faced adversity and how did you face it?

4. Where do you think and/or hope your leadership journey is taking you?

5. What does being a serving leader mean to you?

Chapter Two

The Qualities of Serving Leaders

Several years ago, I was at a school and I was nervous to go in to talk to the students. It was a little scary!

Would they like me?

Would they like my stories?

Would they fall asleep while I was talking?

There was a window next to the door, so I could look in at them. They were fidgeting. They were talking. They were poking each other. And then, from inside the room I heard...

"And now boys and girls, welcome Mr. Kelly."

I walked into the room to face the most hostile and volatile of audiences possible...

Five-year olds!

I was at an at-risk elementary school that my Kiwanis club sponsored to read to kindergarteners. The school is considered at-risk because many of the kids were from one-parent or no-parent homes. No-parent homes means that they are being raised by someone other than their mother or father such as an aunt, grandmother, older sister, or family friend. Some of the children are homeless.

I strode into the room to the audible gasps of the little people sitting crisscross applesauce on the floor and went to the reader's chair, which was designed for a five-year old.

I sat down and said "Hi, boys and girls. I am Mr. Kelly and I am from the Kiwanis Club. I am here to read to you today. I brought three books, all by Dr. Seuss. Does anybody like Dr. Seuss?"

Most of the hands went up. Then some went back down. A few more came back up about half-way and stayed there. It seemed like Dr. Seuss was going to be a good bet.

One little girl still had her hand up. "Yes, sweetie, do you have a question?"

"I like Cat in the Hat!" she said enthusiastically.

I hadn't brought Cat in the Hat that day so I thought I might be in trouble.

A little boy to the left, in an Atlanta Falcons t-shirt, had his hand up. "Do you have a question?" I asked him.

"We have three cats!"

Ahhhh, what? I looked over to the teacher for help, but she had her face buried in her hands in some sort of self-induced coma. I was on my own.

I decided to start with my favorite Dr. Seuss book, the one I read to my daughters: Green Eggs and Ham.

I started reading, "I am Sam."

"I am Sam."

"Sam, I am."

"That Sam I am, that Sam I am, I do not like that Sam I am."

And the kids were at rapt attention.

Just like you, hoping I will share more pages from the book, right?

Not exactly. But I did read on about the mouse in the house. And then I read "I will not eat them here or there, I will not eat them…"

"Anywhere!" the kids shouted.

How cool, audience participation!

I continued, "I do not like green eggs and ham, I do not like them…"

"Sam, I am!" the kids shouted even louder. This was becoming fun!

So, I went on about the fox in the box, the train in the rain, and the boat and the goat, and all of the other places that the guy who doesn't like green eggs and ham (we never learn his name) says he will not eat them. The kids kept shouting "Anywhere" and "Sam, I am" as I read each page. They were getting louder and louder and more excited. Soon the first-grade teacher from across the hall came in to ask if I could quiet the children down.

"Are you kidding me?" I exclaimed. "I'm on a roll here!"

I finally got to the point where he agrees to eat the green eggs and ham if Sam will leave him alone. The next page has no words on it, just the guy holding a fork with one of the eggs dangling off it. If there were words, based on his expression, I think it would have been, "Ehw."

And then he eats the egg and he loves it! In fact, he loves it so much that he will eat them in all the places that he said he wouldn't. He finishes the book by saying "I do so love green eggs and ham. Thank you, thank you…" and all the kids said "Sam, I am." And I was hooked. I have been reading to those kids now for more than 20 years.

Well, not the same kids. I hope that original group has graduated from high school by now. The kids are so important to me that I have read to them after surgeries, between meetings, on bad weather days, and even on the way to the airport.

I work with a wonderful teacher named Ms. G. and I don't want to disappoint her kids. Some of them have a lot of disappointments and challenges. I, and the other members of my Kiwanis Club, serve as role models. Most of our Kiwanis readers are men and they treat the teachers, most of whom are women, with respect. We show up from work, smelling of nothing other than after shave or toothpaste.

We care about them.

I remember one little girl from a few years ago. Her name was Amanda and she was five when I started reading to her class. She told me that she got home every day at 3:30 p.m. and no adult was home until 7:00 p.m.! My wife and I didn't let our daughter stay home alone that long until she was 12 or 13 and she had a cell phone, a security system, and four attack cats to protect her.

In Amanda's case, the adult who came home at 7:00 p.m. was her mom's boyfriend. Her mom did not get home until 9:00 p.m. While there was no suspicion of anything inappropriate going on there, those are the types of situations that can turn bad. And fast.

This is just one of the types of opportunities that are available to you to make a difference. The kids need you! And they love it when high school and college students come to read because you are in school just like they are. When you come to read, you are like a rock star. You can drive a car. You can come and go as you please. And you have all kinds of money. Well, to kindergarteners you have all kinds of money.

This is what being a serving leader means. Making a commitment and following through on it. Being a role model. Making a difference in any way that you can.

Thoughts on being a Serving Leader

Serving leadership is not a new idea but is one that some of the great visionary leaders and thinkers of the world have commented upon.

"Everyone can be great. Because anybody can serve. You only need a heart full of grace. A soul generated by love." Dr. Martin Luther King, Jr. (1929-1968)

> I think Dr. King was saying that our greatness will be determined by our service. Service is the legacy we leave behind in school, in our families, in our lives. The work of Dr. King continues to this day because of his heart and soul. It is paid forward in many ways, including the holiday in his honor on the third Monday of January. The King Center in Atlanta calls it, "A Day On, Not A Day Off". It is a day to serve in Dr. King's honor.

"If you can't feed one hundred people, then feed just one." Saint Teresa of Calcutta (1910-1997)

This tells us that little things mean a lot. I am a proponent of service big and small. It is amazing how those things can come together. Mother Teresa won the Nobel Peace Prize in 1979, which came with a one-million-dollar cash award. Nobel laureates are usually lauded at a huge banquet in Oslo, Norway. Mother Teresa asked the organizers how much it cost to put on the banquet. When she was told $192,000, she asked that the banquet be canceled and the money be given to her to feed the hungry of India. She said $192,000 could feed thousands of people for a year in Calcutta.

Mother Teresa was already getting one million dollars! $192,000 is not a small amount, but how many of us would have taken the banquet? I'm guessing the answer is everyone.

In fact, it is the only time that a banquet was not held in the honor of the Peace Prize laureate because Mother Teresa felt a little bit more would mean a lot.

Whenever you serve, do it with joy and make a difference in any way that you can.

"I shall pass through this world but once. Any good therefore that I can do or any kindness that I can show to any human being, let me do it now. Let me not defer or neglect it, for I shall not pass this way again." Mahatma Gandhi (1869-1947)

You never know when you will come upon an opportunity to serve so be ready to seize it! The little kindness that you may show someone today could change their life.

I was a Cub Scout when I was a young boy. My mom was the den mother. She was an example for me. As she led a group of small boys through the various requirements for badges, I got to see the heart of a serving leader.

I remember going to a nursing home at Christmas time in my Cub Scout uniform and singing carols for the residents. Not all the residents were able to come down to hear us. As we were leaving, we had to walk past some of the residents' rooms. I recall one elderly gentleman sitting in his room, in a chair near the doorway. His bald head was covered with bumps, kind of like big pimples, but not exactly, and he had his face in his hands. I was only eight or nine at the time, yet I couldn't help but feel like I should say something to him. Maybe reach out and give him a hug. Try to make his life a little bit better.

I did nothing. I was afraid. Here was a man, clearly hurting, and I sensed it. Yet, I did nothing.

"What if he wants to be left alone?" I asked myself.

"Maybe he doesn't like singing," I thought.

I will never know, because I never reached outside of myself and opened myself up to the opportunity to serve.

And I never passed that way again.

What about you? Have you ever seen an opportunity to serve and avoided it? If you didn't avoid it, did you ever ignore it? Was it out of fear?

Some think that when you get outside of your comfort zone and put a piece of yourself out there to help someone else, they may reject your overture, or worse yet, take advantage of you. You rarely get a positive return from your service efforts, so why bother?

Because a serving leader is willing to put one's self out there, to try to make a difference. Even if you may not pass this way again, the person you help may. Hopefully they will take your kindness and pay it forward.

"For even the Son of Man did not come to be served, but to serve others, and to offer Himself as a sacrifice for many" Mark 10:45

Serving leadership is not a new idea! It goes back thousands of years and even Jesus acknowledged that His life was not about being served, but to serve others. He made the ultimate sacrifice. While most of us are not called to do that, some are. We all can put others first and lead by the example of not doing it for our own benefit or edification, but to make a difference in the lives of those we meet.

"I believe...that every human mind feels pleasure in doing good to another." Thomas Jefferson (1743-1826)

One of the great rewards of serving is that it feels good! We get a chance to make a difference in the lives of others and either we see the results, receive thanks, or know that our efforts are being put to good use. It brings me joy to serve and have a feeling of accomplishment.

"As my mother says, 'You give back, you don't give up.' You can always choose to help others. If you do, it will change you." Susan Ford (1957-)

Susan Ford is the daughter of former U.S. President and First Lady Gerald and Betty Ford and is an author and former chair of the board of directors of the Betty Ford Center, a treatment facility for individuals with substance dependence. She was very close to her mother and is talking about paying it forward in the quote above.

Mrs. Ford was a very open person and publicly shared her health challenges and battle with alcoholism in a way that few in the public eye had done previously. Within weeks after becoming First Lady, Mrs. Ford underwent a mastectomy for breast cancer. Her openness about her disease raised awareness and many more women sought treatment for something many had been reluctant to talk about.

In 1978, Mrs. Ford's family held an intervention with her because of her alcohol and opioid analgesics (a prescription painkiller) usage, so she sought treatment. Mrs. Ford went public with her addictions and stay in rehab.

Today, we are used to celebrities and people in the public eye going in and out of rehab. At that time, however, famous people kept these kinds of things hush-hush and didn't admit that they had a problem. Not only did Betty Ford go public, but she also founded the Betty Ford Center for the treatment of chemical dependency and stayed active with the center as chair of the board of directors until 2005.

It is a choice to be a serving leader. It changes how you look at people and at the world. It is part of everything you do.

"It's not about what you have or what you've accomplished. It's about who you've lifted up and made better. It's about what you've given back." Denzel Washington (1954-)

Serving leaders can be found everywhere, including in entertainment. I found this Denzel Washington quote after I read an article in a magazine celebrating his 20 years of service as the national spokesperson for the Boys and Girls Clubs of America. The article spoke of his dedication to the organization and his time spent as a boy at the Boys Club in his neighborhood. He said that students, mentors, teachers, and coaches at the club helped to make him the man he is. His philanthropy is giving back through donations and service to his church, military organizations, colleges, universities, and more.

I believe in giving back and, when I joined a Kiwanis Club, I supported the youth organizations, Key Club and Circle K, that had given so much to me. In doing so I found that service builds certain leadership qualities and characteristics in people. I saw how the students I worked with, as an advisor, grew as people and leaders. The experiences helped me see how serving others and leadership roles can come together.

I have identified four areas that I believe define the qualities of serving leaders:

1. **Dignity of the Individual**: how we treat others and how we look at them, our attitude towards their situations and circumstances, and what we do when interacting with people;

2. **Sacrifice and Integrity**: the way that we lead in school, work, organizations, and life; what our approaches are in choosing to be a leader and the reason why we do it;

3. **Recognition**: knowing who we are and how we are going to get to where we want to be in service and leadership; and

4. **Responsible Stewardship**: what we do with what has been given to us in terms of resources, opportunities, and the people we lead.

In the chapters that follow, each of these areas will be further broken down into different qualities that visionary serving leaders possess.

Discussion/Reflection Questions

1. Who is a serving leader, either that you know personally or someone of note that you respect, that has had an impact on your life?

2. When have you had to make sacrifices, as a leader, for others?

3. How have you given back, or paid it forward, for something someone has done for you?

4. What makes you feel good about serving others?

Chapter Three

Dignity of the Individual

Serving leadership is about working with others and recognizing their abilities. It elevates people without judging them. Dignity of the individual is all about how you treat others. I think one of the ways we show dignity to others is by being a good listener.

Leaders Listen

Have you ever been in a conversation with someone, but were not really listening to them? All the time, right? Or maybe you were half listening, because you were thinking, "As soon as they shut up, here is what I am going to say…."

What if they suddenly looked at you and asked, "What did I just say?"

I've been married 30 years. I have heard that a lot!

Recently, I was concerned about my hearing, so I made an appointment with an audiologist. During the exam, she ran me through a series of tests. One of them was just like something they did when I was a kid: she put headphones on me and played tones in each of my ears at varying sound levels to check my hearing.

I passed with flying colors! This led my audiologist to ask, "Why did you come in today? There is nothing wrong with your hearing."

To which I replied, "Well, sometimes, when my wife talks…"

Yeah, I really said this.

"…I don't hear what she is saying."

The audiologist looked at me, put one hand on her hip, and then cocked her head to the side saying, through body language only, "Really?"

That made me realize I needed to be a better listener, especially with my wife. Advances in technology have helped. The ability to pause live television may have saved our marriage!

What people have to say is important to them and it needs to be important to you. Regardless of how crazy their ideas are, you may find a nugget of something you can use. Much like the excited student who comes to you and says, "We should build a Death Star on campus. Yeah, and then have light saber battles in there and fight against the dark side of the force. On Halloween, we could have little kids come on campus, trick or treat in it and then get in the Millennium Falcon and fly around the universe."

That all sounds pretty cool, doesn't it? I always have students in my audiences who whisper, "We *should* build a Death Star on campus!"

From a practical standpoint, though, it is not realistic. That could cause you to tune the person out. By paying attention, though, you could pick up on something great.

"I don't know about the Death Star and all that stuff but tell me more about your trick or treat idea."

A quick activity to illustrate the need for focused listening is to ask students to get into pairs or slightly larger groups. Tell them that they have 30 seconds to talk about anything they want to.

The caveats are that each person in the pair or the group will talk at the same time and they need to talk for the whole time. They can talk about anything they want. This works well if they are seated at tables and can just talk into the middle, not focusing on anyone in particular. After 30 seconds, call time, and ask them if they actually learned anything in the activity. They usually will have heard something, but the cacophony of noise makes quality listening difficult. It points out how important is to be a focused listener.

I want you to be one of the best listeners in the world. I want you to be like the comedian Beck Bennett who played the deadpan moderator in the 2013 AT&T "It's Not Complicated" commercial series who sits and talk to a focus group of little kids. He was a great listener because he would be scripted in order to get the children talking, but the kids were not scripted. Bennett would talk to them until the producers felt they had enough to make a good commercial.

One of my favorites was when one of the kids said, "Knock, knock."

Bennett asks, "Who's there?"

The kid responds with, "Queen."

Bennett: "Queen who?"

Kid: "Queen my dishes, please."

They chuckle, but the camera moves in on another little boy with a puzzled look on his face. The fog quickly clears and he says, "CLEAN."

And the joke teller responds with, "It's 'queen' to make it funny."

Bennett looks at the joke teller, points to the second kid and says, "He doesn't get it."

Makes me laugh every time!

My all-time favorite of these commercials involved four kids sitting at a table when one little girl says something delightful. Bennett looks at her and asks, "Are you competing for cutest kid right now?"

"Yes," she says.

Bennett replies, "And what place are you in?"

She thought for a moment and said, "Kindergarten?"

And our moderator smiles and says, "That's adorable!"

Great things can happen when you listen. People will open up and share with you if they feel that you genuinely care about what they have to say.

Leaders play well with others

Serving leaders work well with others and play nice in life's sandbox. But, when they don't, conflict occurs. Most people, unless they are a football player or into mixed martial arts, do not like conflict. Yet, we encounter it every day and from a lot of different sources. Here are a few I have compiled from audiences over the years:

- Cultural, political, religious, or racial differences
- Different opinions and agendas
- Someone trying to do everything themselves
- Other people in a group not contributing or carrying their weight
- A couple's romantic relationship negatively impacting others within the group or organization
- Talking behind someone's back
- Stress
- Being tired
- Being "hangry" (thank you Snickers® for those images!)

The worst conflict initiators are those people who get up every morning, go to the fridge, and pour themselves a great big glass of "Hater-ade." You know them, the people who are just waiting to hate on you the minute you come into view.

A serving leader does not shy away from conflict, in fact, the leader confronts it. I asked a friend of mine, Dr. Jennifer Hughes, a professor of industrial psychology at Agnes Scott College in Decatur, GA, if I could use the modes, or styles, of managing conflict that she shared during a convention workshop a few years ago. I love Dr. Hughes' explanations (following in italics) and have added some interpretations of my own.

1) *The **Avoiding** mode of managing conflict is characterized by low assertiveness of one's own interests and low cooperation with the other party. This is the "hiding the head in the sand" – or the "Ostrich Method" response. Although avoidance can provide some short-term stress reduction from the rigors of conflict, it does not really change the situation. Thus, its effectiveness is often limited. Avoidance does, however, have its place if the issue*

is trivial, people need to cool down, or the opponent is very powerful and hostile.

Sticking your head in the sand can work in the short term, but what happens when you turn away from a conflict and try to ignore it? It usually gets bigger and worse. So, this is not really an effective way of dealing with conflict.

2) *The **Accommodating** mode entails cooperating with the other party's wishes while not asserting one's own interests. If people see accommodation as a sign of weakness, it does not bode well for future interactions. However, it can be an effective reaction when you are wrong, the issue is more important to the other party, or you want to build goodwill.*

If you want to live to fight another day, then this is the approach you want to take. I liken it to marriage! (I can't talk about this style without thinking about the wedding scene from the movie "The Princess Bride" when the officiant says, in his distinctive voice, "Marriage. Marriage is what brings us together today.")

The problem with this is that if one party is always giving in to the other, they will eventually tire of it and then draw a line in the sand while saying, "Don't step over this." And what if the other person or group does step over the line? That is when things can turn very ugly in relationships, organizations, and work.

3) *The **Competing** mode tends to maximize assertiveness for your own position and minimize cooperative responses. In doing so, you tend to frame the conflict in strict win-lose terms. Full priority is given to your own goals, facts, or procedures. The competing style holds promise when you have a lot of power, you are sure of your facts, the situation is truly win-lose, or you will not have to interact with the other party in the future.*

I call this the "Survivor" approach to dealing with conflict – "Outwit. Outlast. Outplay." The thing is if you must win at all costs, then that means someone must lose. And if one side in a relationship or organization is always losing, there will come a time when they decide to pick up their marbles and go home. This is how groups fracture and fall apart, so I do not think it is a very effective method of handling relationships and conflict.

4) *The **Compromise** mode combines intermediate levels of assertiveness and cooperation. Thus, it is itself a compromise between pure Competition and pure Accommodation. Compromise places a premium on determining rules of exchange between the two parties. Also, compromise does not always result in the most creative response to conflict. Compromise is not so useful for resolving conflicts between individuals on different levels of an organization, because the weaker party may have little to offer the stronger party. However, it is a sensible reaction to conflict stemming from scarce resources.*

I call this "The Congress" style of dealing with conflict. Two parties tend to start out on two far ends of an issue and then meet somewhere in the "muddle" [not a typo] because whatever they are trying to accomplish, they seem to just make things worse. As the definition above points out, compromising does not always lead to the best result, just one everybody can live with.

It seems to be in the nature of many leaders to try to work for compromises. I have a few interactives and role-playing games that I use and, even though they have a definitive result, most people tend to try to compromise rather than work through to the best solution.

When I was CKI District Administrator, I would see this dynamic at work and sometimes had to guide the students to make a firm decision that worked best, even if it did not make everyone happy. This is an important lesson in leadership: just because what you wanted did not happen does not mean that your voice was not heard. Unlike the Competing style, sometimes the group will make a decision that is contrary to what you hoped would happen.

5) *The* **Collaboration** *mode maximizes both assertiveness and cooperation with the hope that an integrative agreement will occur that fully satisfies the interests of both parties. Emphasis is put on a win-win resolution in which there is no assumption that someone must lose something. Rather it is assumed that the solution to the conflict can leave both parties in a better condition. Ideally, collaboration occurs as a kind of problem-solving exercise. It probably works best when the conflict is not intense and when each party has information that is useful to the other.*

This is the best way to resolve conflicts and issues and come to decisions. Seeking a win-win situation means laying all the cards on the table and fully communicating. You work through to the best solution and may find that any conflicts or disagreements are akin to apples-and-oranges discussions where you and the other party are not even talking about the same thing! When my wife and I have a disagreement, it is usually of that type and, after fully communicating, we realize we can work together to solve each of the points that need addressing.

Seek collaboration and you will find much more satisfaction with the decisions that are made and the results that you and/or your group will achieve.

I have some additional ways of dealing with conflict that I call **Dave's 5 Concepts of Conflict Resolution**.

1. **If you have a problem with someone and do not take it to them, then it can't be very significant.** This was shared with me when I was the Wisconsin-Upper Michigan Circle K District Governor and it has stuck with me for more than 30 years. If you have a conflict or issue with someone, then who is the only person that can solve it? Them!

   Too many times we talk to everyone else but the person with whom we have an issue and then wonder why it doesn't get resolved or go away. It's like the "Telephone" game we played as kids. The first person whispers a word or phrase to the person next to them and the second person whispers it to the third person, until the word or phrase has passed from person to person to the other end of the line. When the last person repeats out loud what they heard, it sounds nothing like what it started out as. In my presentations I point to a person on one side of the room designating them as the first person in the line. I briefly share my conflict with them ("I think Sarah is mad at me") and by the time it gets around to the other side of the room the last person looks at me and might say, "I understand you had something to do with the Great Depression!" First of all, that happened way before I was born and, second of all, it is illustrative of what happens when we do not take our problem directly to the person with whom we have an issue.

   Take the issue to the person and discuss it. Or else get over it. This should be done one-on-one. You don't want the other party to feel ganged up on. You might bring an impartial third party to help mediate but they must clearly be neutral in the dispute.

2. **Deal with conflict one on one: praise in public, criticize in private.** Most people like to be praised publicly for something they have done for the group or an

accomplishment they have achieved. Not all, but most. There are some people who are not comfortable with public recognition, but they will usually accept it.

No one wants to be criticized in public, however. It can be embarrassing, debilitating, and make them feel unwanted or unworthy. Some people who are criticized in public may lose their cool and explode in a dramatic flourish of hysteria that can't be taken back and probably won't be forgotten by others. A serving leader should have enough respect for the dignity of individuals to deliver criticism in private. "Hey, do you have a few minutes to talk after the meeting?" Then calmly discuss the issue or concern without accusation and offer to help resolve the matter. It is possible they may still lose it, but at least it will only be with you and not the whole group. If that happens, reassure them everything that was discussed is just between the two of you… and keep it that way!

3. **Use the 3 C method: compliment, criticize, compliment.**
   I call this the compliment sandwich, where you praise a person on both sides of a critique. Such as, "Hey, Ronnie, you have so many great ideas, but when you talk out of turn it disrupts the meeting, so raise your hand when you have input and then we can all focus on your awesomeness!" See? Compliment, criticize, compliment.

   Unlike my high school English teacher, Miss Due, who, on the first day of class our senior year, saw Ronnie being disruptive and said to him, "You sir, are a creep, sir." And Ronnie was disruptive the entire semester. Someone did point out once that Miss Due did use the compliment sandwich by calling him "sir" on both ends of the statement but calling someone a creep in the middle of the sandwich is not what I had in mind.

4) **Separate the person from the position.** Who you are is not what you do. You may be a great member and get elected to a leadership position. Or maybe you are very popular, and everyone thinks you would make a good club president. Or maybe you missed the meeting when nominations and elections were held, and you got elected to a leadership role you weren't expecting but you decided to go ahead and give it your best.

And maybe you found out that you were in over your head and not cut out for this role. Maybe you have such a heavy academic load that you cannot devote the time necessary to successfully fulfill the duties of the position. You may have family stuff happening or work that gets in the way. This does not mean you are not a good person or a bad member.

Perceptions, however, sometimes turn into realities and others may look unfavorably upon you because of your performance in a leadership role. Is that fair? No. But, we sometimes do this when we see other people in this circumstance.

Work with people to help them be better in their positions and, if they still don't get it, give them an opportunity to either ask for a second person to work with like an Assistant Secretary or possibly step away from the role.

Separate the person from the position so you can keep them as a member and as a friend.

The next concept pairs with this and helps the person find a graceful way out...

5) **Address the situation by asking a direct question.** I came up with this idea during my first year as the District

Administrator of Georgia CKI. We had a member of our district board who was not fulfilling his role as Lt. Governor (remember when I talked about being an LTG in the first chapter?). The Governor needed to either get him on track or ask him to resign so that someone else could fill the position. I suggested she meet with him and lay out all responsibilities that had been covered during training. She would explain that he needed to do them and she would work with him to come up with a plan for doing so.

During the meeting, she gave him the list of duties and asked if he thought he could fulfill them all. He pointed out three or four of them that he liked and felt he could do, but there were five or six that he didn't want to do or didn't feel he could complete successfully.

She calmly told him that he was required to do all of them and if he couldn't, then they needed to come up with a resolution to the situation. She asked, "Given that these are the requirements, do you want to continue as Lt. Governor?"

After thinking for a few moments, he said, "If I have to do all of these things, then I don't think I want to stay in the position."

He resigned and our Governor appointed a new person in his place who did a great job finishing out the term.

No fuss, no muss. She addressed the situation with a direct question and he eliminated himself in a way that was respectful and allowed him to continue as a member of the organization without embarrassment.

Conflict does not have to hurt. If serving leaders work at it, they can come up with solutions that work for everyone!

Serving leaders do not think of themselves first, selfish leaders do. Not that all ambitious people are selfish, but the heart of the serving leader needs to be evident.

Leaders put others above self
&
Leaders have an awareness of the needs, desires, and dreams of others

Serving leaders put others above self. They have an awareness of the needs, desires, and dreams of others. I think these two qualities go hand in hand. If you look to fulfill the needs of others first, to help them achieve their dreams and desires, then you are a serving leader.

A great example of this is shown in a Guinness® beer commercial where six wheelchair-bound guys are playing basketball. They are pretty intense, shooting the ball, dribbling up the court, banging into each other. Several fell over in their chairs. As the commercial progresses, a voice narrates over the action, "Dedication. Loyalty. Friendship."

When one of the players makes a basket that must have been the winning shot, the camera focuses in on another player who says, "You're getting better at this." The camera then turns to show five of the guys standing up and getting out of their chairs. The sixth one cannot. The narrator finishes with, "The choices we make reveal the true nature of our character."

This is serving leadership. The friends of the one guy using the wheelchair wanted to play ball with their buddy, so they decided to play his way. They put him above themselves, they considered his needs and his desire to "ball with his boys."

As a serving leader, when you consider the dignity of the individual, recognize that it is a distinction between *service* and *serve us*.

If you are asking "What's in it for me?", then you are asking the wrong question.

Discussion/Reflection Questions

1. Do you consider yourself to be a good listener? Why or why not?

2. Have you ever found yourself in a situation where someone you were talking to did not really appear to be listening or paying attention? How did that make you feel? Did you express your feelings to them?

3. Think of some conflicts you have been involved in or asked to help with. How do you approach them? What kind of results have you had in trying to resolve them?

4. When was a time where you put the needs or desires of another person or group ahead of yours? What happened, either positive or negative?

Chapter Four

Sacrifice and Integrity

If you are someone who cares *how* you lead, not just *that* you lead, then you are a serving leader!

Serving leaders are the kind of people who lead in a particular way. They know they are leading, but the welfare of the group and its members is more important to them than their stature. They make sacrifices, they take risks, and they can be trusted to put what is best for everyone first, even ahead of what may be best for them. That takes integrity, which I consider to be one of the most important values a person can have.

Integrity can be tough. I spent 25 years in the mortgage business and the biggest challenge I saw was in trusting the documents that were presented to support the biggest financial obligation some people would have in their entire lifetimes: a house! There are rules in lending money. Some call them guidelines, I called them rules carved in granite. You cannot have wiggle room when it comes to property values or a person's income and credit.

I decided early on that I would never compromise, never skirt the edges, that things would stand on their own. This meant that a lot of people would not be able to buy their dream home or refinance their bills to make providing for their family easier. I believe that integrity is not negotiable and I was never willing to sacrifice my integrity or my whole career for the sake of the commission that may come on any given deal.

People in my industry knew that. So, in those cases where there might be some gray area on a person's credit, or one of the rules in granite might need to be expanded as an exception, more often than not, I was able to make a case and my lending partners trusted me. They knew I had the best interests of my customers and my lenders at heart. I worked to create a win-win scenario, as I discussed in the last chapter, without compromising my integrity, my customer's financial well-being, or the standards of the investment institution making the loan. It is a service industry and the needs of everyone on all sides had to be met. The sacrifice on my part was many times working through problems and taking on the stress and pressure until a viable solution could be found, in most cases, without the client even knowing there was an issue. That is where experience and a whole lot of trust, built up over time, served me and the people I worked with well.

Sacrifice and integrity will serve you well, too. Even though you may not have as much experience with whatever you are doing, you earn goodwill through your actions, how you treat people, and the things that you do.

Leaders are willing to take risks

A serving leader has a willingness to take risks. Now, I am not talking about bungee jumping off the student center (and please don't!), but rather risks that will benefit your group, organization, or campus. You must be willing to put yourself on the line, like I did for my clients. If I could solve a problem or an issue without having to take it to my client causing them worry, then I would do my best to accomplish that. I put myself on the line.

How would you do that for your organization? You lead from out front. Let the slings and arrows hit you, not your members, no matter what you may face. Understand that obstacles are not roadblocks, but barriers to be overcome.

However, you may have to stick your neck out to overcome those barriers.

I believe that limitations can be overcome. Throughout history, people have shown that physical, mental, and financial limitations would not hold them back. My experience has shown me that most limitations are self-imposed. If you believe that you cannot do something, then you are right. You must believe that you will succeed, no matter what. Success at the end may look different than what you expected, but it will still look pretty good. I had no idea how to become a professional speaker, but I dove in anyway.

I have a quote that has hung on my office wall for over 30 years by German philosopher Johan Wolfgang von Goethe (1749-1832):

"Whatever you can do, or dream you can, begin it. Boldness has genius, power, and magic in it."

I have taken this to mean that we are to go after those things that are important to us, even if the moment is not perfect. There is energy and excitement that comes from anything new. It motivates us to push on and work to achieve our goals and dreams. The reality is that there are no perfect moments, so get started, do something new. Barriers are to be climbed over, gone around, plowed through, and overcome. Take a risk!

Leaders build up others

When people see the kinds of risks and sacrifices that you are willing to make, then you become a builder of other people and communities.

I think of a student leader named Devin when I think about building up other people. I met Devin at our fall membership retreat (FMR) when she was a first-year student. She had just joined CKI about two months earlier and this was her first event. She was very quiet and introverted, so I struck up a conversation with her.

"Hi, I'm Dave. What's your name?"

"Devin."

"Where do you go to school, Devin?"

"Wesleyan College."

"That's a great school and a great club. Have fun at FMR and let me know if we can help you in anyway."

She went off to be with the other members of her club. I was meeting a lot of new students, so I am not sure how much I thought about Devin - until Saturday night, that is.

Since our retreat was over Halloween weekend, we had a costume party and contest as our Saturday evening activity. Devin was dressed in a really cool outfit and a lot of people encouraged her to enter the competition. She made the finals and won!

I saw her the next day and congratulated her. She told me she had a great time and was thinking about running for club president in the spring. I told her that I thought that was a great idea and wished her luck.

I didn't see Devin again until our spring convention and, when I did, I asked her if she had run for and won club president.

She very quietly told me "I did run, but Abby also ran and she won."

Abby was a junior and was amazing.

"Well, Abby will be a really good president."

Devin said, "I know."

Then I said, "You know, if you still want to have a leadership role, you could run for the district board."

"Really? But I've never been a club officer?"

"You don't have to have ever had a club office. And we'll teach you everything you need to know."

"Maybe..." was her response. And I encouraged her to think about it.

That night I told the story of how I ran for Lt. Governor at my first Key Club convention by raising my hand and saying, "I'll do it" and it leading me into Circle K, my career as a mortgage broker, then to Atlanta, and eventually meeting my wife.

During our nomination process that night, Devin was nominated for Lt. Governor. Her club was completely behind her and helped her create a platform and prepare for caucus. Although she was still a little quiet, she had a certain confidence that shone through.

The election for that position was at-large and we could have up to five winners. The caveat was that a candidate had to receive 50% plus one of the votes cast. We elected four Lt. Governors at that convention and Devin was one of them.

She did a great job working with the clubs in the southern part of Georgia, making visits and publishing newsletters. And she was coming out of her shell. She was so good, in fact, that the following January I called her and asked if she was thinking about running for Governor.

"Really? Do you think I could do it?"

I told her "Absolutely! I think you would be great!", which I did, plus, I didn't really like the guy who was running.

OK, that's a joke. I always worked to recruit good candidates so our members would have choices. No election rigging here!

Devin was an outstanding Governor. At the beginning of her term, she gave a presentation on her vision for the year to her board of 15-20 students and advisors and wowed everyone. She was becoming such an impressive speaker that the Kiwanis District Governor, Lillie, asked her to speak in front of around 500 attendees during the very formal Governor's Banquet on Saturday night during the Kiwanis District Convention. This was unprecedented as the youth leaders usually spoke during the Saturday morning business session.

Lillie and Devin had formed a special bond, in part because of their backgrounds. Lillie was both the first female and the first African American governor in the history of the Georgia Kiwanis District. Devin's parents were from Jamaica and she was Georgia Circle K's first governor of color. It was a historic time and Devin gave one of the best speeches I have ever heard from a student leader in any setting.

Devin continued her outstanding work and had a great Dr. Seuss themed convention. Devin's mother, Keva, was in attendance and she beamed at her daughter's accomplishments. Keva's birthday was Sunday of the convention, March 2, the same as Dr. Seuss. So, we had a birthday celebration for her before Devin's farewell address. Devin was fully beyond quiet mode by this point.

Circle K International awarded Devin and Georgia with the Distinguished District Award that summer after her term ended. Although it was our fifth straight, it was very special. Only three of the 30 districts were awarded that year and Devin had come so far as a person and leader that I was especially proud to join her on stage to receive the honor.

She graduated and went on to earn a Master of Public Administration. She got a job in the fundraising department at a museum after graduation. She moved up in leadership within her department and got to know many of the movers and shakers of the area. She left the museum for a short time to work with a service-based company in the private sector, but found it was not what she was looking for.

In the summer of 2013, I had a speaking engagement near where Devin lived, so she came to meet me at the airport before my return flight. We caught up over coffee and she told me she had applied for a position as the Volunteer Coordinator for a large food bank. I thought this would be perfect for her, a great use of her talents and abilities. She asked me if I was willing to be a reference and, of course, I was thrilled to do so.

I got a call a couple of days later for the reference and gushed about Devin, her leadership abilities, her skills in communication and organization, and more. Devin called me the next day to let me know she got the job!

"Of course you did", I said, "I am sure it was all due to my reference!"

She took the job and is still there serving the people of her community. She is a true success story and a great example of what can happen when you seek to build people and communities.

Serving leadership is for anyone. When our daughter was in the 5th grade, one of her fellow students was being bullied regarding her appearance. The girls had each other since they were in pre-school. The bullying became so bad, though, that Katie decided to do something about it. She got together with her best friend, who was also in the class, and they decided to make R. their friend and a part of their cool kids' group. Katie told the other cool kids that if they didn't want to be friends with R., then they couldn't be friends with her. Because of this, R. grew in self-esteem and became much more confident in herself.

Later, R.'s mom sent an email to us and to Katie's best friend's parents:

> "I wanted to thank you for your daughters standing up for R. at school the last few weeks. She has been bullied this year and your girls have talked to teachers on her behalf. It means so much to see your strong, young girls doing the right thing even when it could be hard. You are raising tomorrow's leaders with compassionate hearts. R. has thanked them, but please pass along my gratitude as well."

I was so proud of our daughter then and still am as she continues to grow as a serving leader! Elevating the self-esteem of others is one way to build people and communities!

Leaders lift others up without judgment

A serving leader exhibits compassion that lifts up others without judgement.

"Oh, look at these poor wretches! I must serve them because they are unable to serve themselves."

NO! You serve because there is a need, whether short- or long-term.

I heard of a church ministry that provides for low-income people in the community. Parishioners, neighbors, and businesses in the area collected food, toiletries, and school supplies for the families. Everything was brought to the church gymnasium and volunteers gathered to package the items to be distributed. At check-in, every volunteer was given a t-shirt to wear during the packing – because we love to getting t-shirts, right? The real goal was to ensure that everyone would be similarly dressed.

Why was this last point important? Because among the volunteers doing the packing were the families who were going to receive the donations! With everyone wearing the same project t-shirt, it was less obvious who the "needy" were. This allowed the volunteers to show compassion and serve, even if they were tempted to be judgmental. "Can you believe these people can't even afford to buy school supplies for their kids?" is something someone might say to the person next them, unless they were unsure if that person could be from one of the receiving families.

Jesus said, "Truly I tell you, whatever you did for one of the least of these brothers and sisters of mine, you did for me." (Matthew 25:40, *NIV*).

Everyone faces challenges. One in five children face hunger each day. Seven million senior citizens deal with food insecurity. Sometimes families must make decisions about which kids get to wear underwear. Really!

A former member of my Kiwanis club was an elementary school principal. One day a little boy came into her office soaking wet because it was raining, and he had fallen into a puddle. She had a T-shirt and some shorts for him to change into and, much to her surprise, he changed right in her office! An even greater surprise was learning that he was not wearing underwear. When she asked him about it, he told her that his sisters got underwear because they wore dresses to school. The boys in his family did not wear underwear because they could not afford enough for everyone.

She relayed this story to our club and we provided money to buy underwear, socks, and umbrellas to stock the school's emergency closet. How can children focus on learning when they are wearing wet clothes or worried that other kids will find out they have no underwear?

We also collected unwrapped toys for Christmas for some of the families. It wasn't just our club, people in the community also helped. At the time, I was serving as a board member for a mortgage trade association and I saw a great donation opportunity. We had a holiday party every year which was paid for by sponsors looking to get their name and services in front of our broker members. Since there was no charge to attend the party, I asked the board to approve asking members for a donation of an unwrapped toy as the price of admission. We got some pretty cool stuff! And never was there judgment. Just a chance to lift up others.

Leaders lead with integrity in the midst of chaos

Sometimes, chaos comes along. It can bring out the best in people when they step up amidst the chaos. Serving leaders can be trusted to lead with integrity during these times.

It was three days before Christmas, 2004. Our daughter had just turned three a few weeks earlier. We were excited about opening presents and going on our annual "Jammies and Lights Tour" in which we would drive through local neighborhoods (while wearing our PJs) to see how people had decorated their houses.

On this particular night, or I should say morning, I woke up to someone pounding on our front door at 4:00 a.m. I assumed someone had too much holiday cheer and was at the wrong house. I tried to ignore it, but the noise did not go away. So, I got out of bed, went to the front door, and peeked out the window to see who was there. It was a police officer! As soon as he saw me, his eyes got big and he shouted one word…

"FIRE!"

"Oh my gosh, our house is on fire!" is what went through my head. I ran to the front of the house to our daughter's bedroom to get her. In those few moments I realized that I did not smell smoke, nor did I feel any heat. What was going on?

We live on a circle with 19 houses, called patio homes. They are the size of a regular house, but we do not have yards. We have walkways along the side of our homes that lead to a back patio. Some of the units are attached to each other, like ours, and some are free standing.

In my moment of clarity, I went to the window and looked out: 25 to 30 yards away, straight down our driveway, across a little shared access road, two of my neighbor's homes were completely engulfed in flames.

Dia ran in and asked me what was going on. I told her that Gail's and Cindy's houses (houses #1 and #2) were on fire and that we needed to get out. She scooped up our daughter and we went for the front door. As I opened it, I saw that the police officer was still on our porch waiting for us.

"Get out of the circle now!" he said and he jumped onto our fence, climbed over, and began pounding on our neighbor's door.

I recall him being kind of short and the image of his feet kicking over the fence is still with me. So, too, is the fact that he did not leave us until he knew we were out of our house.

We went through our front gate and in those few short moments I saw that two more houses (#3 and #4) were on fire. I was sure that our entire circle was going to burn down.

A firefighter was on top of a ladder hosing down another two houses (#5 and #6) to try to stop the progression of the flames. It looked like he was having success.

We later found out that he had to be taken to the hospital with third degree burns on his legs because he refused to come down until he stopped the fire. He was a true hero and his efforts saved our circle. I also knew, though, that what he was doing meant that the fire department had given up on houses #1, #2, #3, and #4.

We ran down the hill to the entrance of the circle and got out on the main road where several police cruisers sat with engines idling. Gail and Cindy were there, in tears. Dia was crying, our daughter was howling. It was cold, really cold.

Everyone was in pajamas and barefoot. Except for me. Somehow, I managed to put shoes on. I don't know how that happened. I certainly had not been sleeping in them.

Officer Lemke walked over and told us we could sit in his cruiser to keep warm. We got in and everyone was still crying. I wanted to do something and the only thing I could think of was to ask them to hold hands and pray. We prayed for the fire to stop, for the fire fighters, and for the police officers. We prayed for Cindy's dog and cats, because no one had seen them, and we prayed for all the neighbors. This helped everyone to calm down and we sat for a while in the warmth of the cruiser. Eventually, Officer Lemke came to tell us that the fire had been contained and the fire department was going to allow everyone to go into one of the units closest to the circle entrance, away from the devastation. The home belonged to our neighbor, Phil.

A lot of our neighbors were already in Phil's house when we got there. He was making coffee and putting out juice, cereal and anything else he had. His sister was there, too, visiting for the holidays. I don't remember her name, but when we learned she was a Catholic nun, we just called her "Sister Sister."

Most people were talking about their experiences that morning, how they came to know about the fire, what they did to be safe. Others were already on to the "what's next?" of this event.

One of our neighbors, Meg, was from England and was scheduled to fly home to London the next day. She lived in house #4. This was prior to e-tickets sent over cell phones. Somewhere in the wreckage of her house was her plane ticket and her passport. She would be spending Christmas in America.

The couple who owned house #3 were Mr. and Mrs. Baird. They had moved into their home less than a year prior, were retired, and in their mid-70s. I heard Mrs. Baird in the kitchen telling some of our neighbors how they found out about the fire and how grateful she was that they got out and were safe.

I looked over in the corner of the living room and I saw Mr. Baird sitting in a chair, by himself. He was slumped down and he looked ashen, as if all the blood had been drained from his face. He was clearly devastated.

I wanted to do something for him but didn't know what. What could I possibly say in a moment like that? My house had been saved. I walked over to him and he looked up at me. I could see the tears welling up in his eyes. I didn't say anything. I just sat down next to him and took his hand.

We sat there silently for a while, his hand in mine. Eventually the fire department came in and gathered up the affected homeowners to discuss with them what to do next. What I did was small, but Mrs. Baird later told my wife that my gesture really meant a lot to them.

While we were all hunkered down inside Phil's house, my wife was outside. She was the homeowner's association president and decided to deal with the police, the fire department, and especially the media. She did not want the media sticking microphones in the faces of people who had just lost everything. Phil gave her one of his jackets and a pair of his shoes, which were a bit too big for her. It was a funny sight during some serious life-altering things happening.

The fire was all over the news that morning. We could hear the Atlanta traffic helicopters hovering above us. One of the big-time talk radio hosts was the original owner of our house and he was talking about the circle and the fire. Early morning traffic was a mess because the police were not allowing cars to come near our subdivision which was close to a main thoroughfare.

It was also the morning of our annual Kiwanis Holiday Breakfast. Dia had arranged for two of the pastors from our church, Mike and Dean, to deliver the program, a holiday message, at the meeting. We heard from them during the chaos and they told Dia they were trying to get to our subdivision, but the police wouldn't let them through. She told them to go to the Kiwanis meeting, let our members know what was happening, and asked them to pray for our neighbors. They said they would.

By around 9:30 am, most of the excitement was over. The fire department had done all they could. They had stopped the fire at houses #5 and #6 and the flames were out. There was still some smoke, but it was no longer a danger. Friends and family gradually came to pick up the neighbors who had been impacted, since nearly all their vehicles had burned up in their garages.

As the last of the impacted neighbors drove away, several of us were standing outside of Phil's house, looking at the damage and destruction. We turned and saw two men walking around the corner and into the circle: Mike and Dean! They had gone to the Kiwanis meeting and came straight to us on the way back. They still could not drive into the subdivision, but they parked nearby. The police let them through on foot when they explained that they were pastors for several of the homeowners.

Hugs were shared all around, then we made a circle and they prayed for all of us, especially for the affected homeowners, and for a quick recovery for the neighborhood. They pledged the support of the church and, in fact, the church took up a collection on Christmas Eve. They also accepted donations from the community and ultimately collected over $25,000 for our neighbors.

Local businesses also responded, especially the restaurants. Some wanted to send over food, but that was not workable because the victims of the fire were kind of scattered. Dia instead asked for gift cards and directed any food donations to the fire and police stations that had responded.

A lot of people led with integrity that morning:

- The police officer who would not leave our door until we were safely away.
- Officer Lemke who let us sit in his cruiser.
- Someone who was not even there that morning but who had donated a trauma bear to the police department that was, in turn, given to our daughter (and she still has her Lemke Bear).
- The firefighter who would not come down the ladder until the fire was out.
- Our neighbor Phil and Sister Sister who took us all in.
- My wife, standing outside, fielding requests from the police, the fire department, and the media.
- Mike and Dean who did not give up until they got to us.
- Even me when I got everyone to pray in the police car and when I sat with Mr. Baird.

Some led in big ways, others in small ways, but many people were serving leaders that morning.

When you have the heart and attitude of and live as a serving leader, you will step up when the time comes. The response is natural and comes automatically, without thinking. That comes from a willingness to make sacrifices and a commitment to integrity.

Discussion/Reflection Questions

1. Can you think of a time when you took a risk to serve someone else? Did you consider it a big risk or a small one?

2. How have you helped to build up people and/or communities? What did they need and how did you serve them and lift them up?

3. Do you have any examples of situations that you saw, are aware of, or participated in where people served compassionately without judgement?

4. When have you served with integrity? Or without concern for yourself? What was the result?

Chapter Five

Recognition

As a serving leader, you need to know who you are and where you are going. Equally vital are knowing your values, the things that are important to you. Values can be character traits, material things, comforts, necessities, and more. The things we have been taught and our life experiences will influence those things. Values vary from person to person, although when we start to look at the most important core values, we will find common ground with a lot of people.

Leaders have strong, uncompromised values

Knowing what you value is important so that when you are tested you will know how to react. As I mentioned above, one of my most important values is integrity. I believe that integrity is not negotiable. You either have it or you don't. Knowing and believing that has always served me well, especially when I was in the mortgage business. There were many times when I could have cut corners or hidden something that I knew could affect my customer's loan application. I had people who would offer me money to do whatever was necessary to get their deal done.

To me, however, no deal or loan was worth sacrificing my career or my business. I would rather walk away and not do the loan—even though I knew someone else would. Your values need to be like boulders in a stream. They stand firm and the stream bends around them. Of course, the stream may wear the rock down over time. That is why it is important to stand strong and to have uncompromised values. People will try to get you to compromise on things that are important to you. They rarely will come up to you and say, "Give me your integrity!", yet some will try to erode it. "I want your education!" is not likely to be said, but someone may try to convince you to skip an important class to go for coffee, lunch, drinks, a movie, or something else that is important to *them*. You may never face someone who will want to kill you for your faith or religious beliefs, but many people around the world live with that possibility every day. And they stand strong.

When I discuss this with audiences, I ask them to write their top three values on an index card and then exchange it with another person. I also ask them to write their first name on the card. They tell each other why those are their top three and then they keep their partner's card.

After everyone has had a chance to share, I gather them back together so we can talk about the activity and how people will try to take their values from them. They must defend their values and they have an obligation to defend the values of others. I encourage each person to go up to their partner later on and ask, "Do you still have my values? Are you keeping them safe?" That is why it is important to have the first name written on the card as it makes the activity real to each participant.

I once did this activity at the New York Key Club District Leadership Conference. There were over 700 high school students in the room and everyone got into trading and sharing. I was on stage at the front of the room and a girl on the front row had no one with whom to trade. She held her card up to me and I took it. Her name was Aurora and her values were "Friends, Family, and Helping People." She told me why those were important to her. I didn't have a card, but I shared my top three: God, Family, and Community Service. That was in March.

67

In November of that year, I did a retreat for the state boards of Key Club, Circle K, and Kiwanis in New York. During one of the breaks, some of the high school students approached me and asked if I still had that girl's card from the district convention. I reached into my pocket, pulled it out and asked, "Do you mean Aurora's card?" They were amazed!

I carry that card with me every time I do a program. It reminds me of how important it is for me to focus on helping my students be the best they can be and that I need to respect and defend their values.

Serving leaders need to watch out for those who may struggle to defend their values against attack, temptation, or expediency.

Leaders have confidence

I believe confidence is one of the most important qualities a person can possess, and it is absolutely vital for serving leaders. Confidence is a top quality that employers seek and attracts us to someone as a mate.

Yet, many students lack confidence in leadership within themselves and their abilities to be successful in roles of responsibility. When I was District Administrator for CKI, I would encourage outstanding members and club leaders to run for positions on our Georgia district board. Many of them hesitated saying things like, "I don't know enough" or "I am afraid I am going to fail." Remember when I wrote about raising my hand and saying, "I'll do it!"? I had those same thoughts. Yet, I dove in and my entire life has been influenced by that one moment.

I told these students that we would teach them everything

they needed to know and would be by their side throughout the year. Some took a chance and served. And many grew as a result of the experience. Some did not take the chance and I do not know where most of them are today.

So, how do you become a confident leader? Here are four keys:

1) **Be willing to take a chance**. Take chances and raise your hand. Be open to opportunities as they may take you to places you never thought possible and give you experiences of a lifetime. And when things don't go your way or you make mistakes, learn from those experiences. Don't live in the past: leave the past in the past. But, always have a take-away from failures or disappointments.

   Too many people live in regret. I say, "turn your regrets into forgets." Those little voices in your head say things like, "Remember that time you did that stupid thing," or "How about when you embarrassed yourself in front of everyone," or other things you would rather not relive. I get little voices of things that happened in high school! That was a long time ago for me! When those little voices harass me, I focus on something positive.

   Here is an example: I like to think about a day when our track team was going to compete against a conference rival. I ran the two-mile race for our team. Horicon High School had a particularly fast track and I boasted to a friend of mine that I thought I could win my race that day. I took things up a level by adding that if I won, I would roll down the hill from the school to the track. He thought that was a pretty good idea!

   Well, I went out and I won! I climbed to the top of the hill and looked for my friend in the infield. When I saw him, I pointed and shouted. He pointed back and, surrounded by our team, shouted back. I proceeded to roll down the hill like a barrel. I could hear everyone laughing, clapping, and cheering. When I got to the bottom, they patted my back and chanted my name. That was a pretty good day! I would rather think about that day than some of the little regrets that pop up.

Think about your good days to build your confidence!

2) **Face Challenges**. Recognize that obstacles are only temporary barriers to achieving your goal or purpose. Things may get in the way and, when they do, go over them, through them, or around them. Find a way to move past those challenges.

A challenge I continually face, much to my annoyance, are people who underestimate me. In several of my endeavors in life, whether business or personal, I have come up against people who did not think I could do what I set out to do. I even wrote a quote about it in my first book, "If you underestimate me, then that is your problem and my challenge." I take it as motivation when someone underestimates me, not to take joy in proving them wrong, but to achieve what I set out to accomplish.

Even with all that I had previously done, from leadership positions to creating a multi-state mortgage company, many people underestimated me when I set out to become a professional speaker. They told me I wasn't good enough or that no one would hire me. Seriously?

I created a plan for how I would get going and I followed it. What helped a lot was telling myself that I was not going into this trying to make a ton of money. Of course, I needed to do well enough to pay our bills and support my family, but I came to this career with an attitude of service. I set out to inspire people through my programs, to serve their needs, and to glorify God through my talents and abilities. That attitude has taken me far and allowed me to move past challenges and obstacles.

3) **Be willing to work hard and be dedicated**. I have a strong work ethic. I always have. I am not sure where I learned that other than watching my parents and other family members who worked hard. I learned early on that I could compensate for my lack of natural abilities by working hard. That is how I made the varsity basketball team. I knew I was not a great shooter, but I was a ferocious rebounder, and played hard on defense. I was willing to out-work my teammates and the opposition.

That attitude has carried me through work situations, leadership roles, and in my speaking career. Perseverance is a large part and I stick with things until victory comes. Thomas Edison said, "Most people miss opportunity because it is dressed in overalls and looks like work." Hard work and dedication have gotten me through a lot and given me the confidence that I can succeed in almost anything I pursue.

4) **Never quit**. When I was in college, I knew that I wanted to be a professional speaker. I didn't know where to start though. I loved the speaking and training opportunities I had as a student leader and saw many professional speakers that we had hired for our conferences and events. I was not sure where to start or learn what I needed to do to become a speaker.

As I thought about this, it occurred to me that I knew someone who was doing what I wanted to do. He was a Kiwanis family member and a professor of leadership at a college in Texas. We had hired him several times to facilitate our programs and I felt comfortable going to him for advice. I decided to write to him to find out what I needed to do to become a professional speaker, be it graduate school, internships or whatever.

It was a Saturday night in January and I was in my apartment in Oshkosh, WI. I was wearing a tank top and gym shorts—sorry for the visual on that—and I got out my typewriter.

Now, when I say typewriter, I do not mean a personal computer. Those did not exist yet. I also did not have one of those nice IBM Selectric typewriters. The ones with a ball that would pop up and smack the paper with the letters you were typing.

No, I had one of those old fashioned, "Mad Men" style manual typewriters, like Jughead Jones uses in the "Riverdale" TV series. The kind that would ding when you got to the end of a line and you had to smack it to the left in order to do a carriage return. THAT was what I had with which to type my letter.

So, I started writing. I addressed my letter to "The Professor of Leadership." I typed for a little bit and then made a typo. Today we just back space to remove typos or spell check will correct it for us. Even the IBM Selectric had a correction key that would allow one to fix a mistake. My manual typewriter had none of that. So, my options were to use Wite-out® brand correction fluid or start over. I didn't want my letter covered in a bunch of Wite-out® so I ripped the paper out of the typewriter and started over.

I began my letter to the Professor of Leadership again and it wasn't long before I made another typo.

"Aaargh!"

So, I pulled the letter out, crumbled it up, and threw it across the room. I started again, typing slower so as not to make any more mistakes. I finally got through the letter and I read it over. It was good, but not perfect. This was going to be my career, my life, so I wanted it to be perfect.

I worked on the letter for a few more hours and finally, around 2:30 a.m., I rolled the letter out of my typewriter and I read it. This time, it was perfect. Not only was it perfect, but it was hot!

I decided I needed to get it from cold Wisconsin to warm Texas just as fast as I could. I pulled out an envelope and I addressed it to the Professor of Leadership in Texas.

With my future firmly in hand, I ran down the steps of my apartment and I burst out into the night air…

… and I was still in my tank top and gym shorts! [OK, my memory might be a little fuzzy here.]

The nearest mailbox was three miles away.

And I had to walk through three feet of snow.

Uphill.

Both ways!

I made it to the mailbox. I was so excited to send my letter. I reached out and grabbed the handle and…

… the box was frozen shut!

What to do?

As, I stood there in my tank top and gym shorts, I realized that I was holding the hottest letter ever written. If I just took the envelope and touched it to the mailbox, then the ice would magically melt, and I could throw my letter in.

So, that's what I did. The ice melted…I swear to God! [That's strange, a lightning bolt just missed hitting me.]

So, I was set. I was on my way. I was freezing my brains out. I headed home, three miles, through the snow, uphill, the other way.

I got into my apartment, sat down and I waited. After waiting a few minutes, I remembered that there was no mail pick up in Oshkosh, Wisconsin at four in the morning on a Sunday, or in most other places for that matter, and it would be okay if I went to bed.

I waited a few days to hear back and there was nothing. There was no internet, so he couldn't send me an email to let me know he had gotten my letter. And, apparently, they did not have phones in Texas then, even though we had them in Wisconsin.

I had to just wait and check my mailbox every day. I would look in and there would be nothing. Or, there would be junk mail. You know, tuition bill, cable bill, phone bill, stuff I didn't want.

Finally, after two weeks of waiting, I opened the mailbox one day and a golden ray of light shone forth!

INTERLUDE

I told this story at a school in New Jersey one time and two girls on the front row, as if on cue, together sang "Ahhhhhhhhh!"

NOW BACK TO OUR STORY

Anyway, the envelope had a return address in the embossed, raised letterhead that professors get to use. It was from the Professor of Leadership in Texas. And it was thick. Surely that meant it had to be more than one page.

I ran up into my apartment, ripped open the envelope, counted the sheets, and it was Five. Pages. Long.

This had to be it! Everything I need to know to become a professional speaker and expert leadership dude!

I started reading the letter from the Professor of Leadership in Texas. It began with, "Hello, Dave. How are you?"

And I audibly responded with, "I'm doing fine. How are you? Why did it take you two weeks to respond to me? Why am I talking to a piece of paper?"

OK, let me get to the good stuff.

I read down to the next paragraph and he talked about an issue we had when I was International President.

"Oh, you want to talk about that? That thing and that time? Hmmm, okay. Wait, you think we should have done that? Well, I'm not so sure, but all right. Now give me the good stuff."

On to the next paragraph.

"Huh? What? You want to talk about another time and another thing?"

And I flipped through the pages of the letter and realized he had not answered any of my questions at all.

Instead, he had taken five pages to tell me what a horrible student leader I was, that my leadership style was completely wrong, and that Circle K would be better off if I went away and was never heard from again.

Ever have somebody reach down your throat, rip out your heart, and stomp on it right in front of you?

That is what happened to me that day. That letter destroyed my confidence and my dream of becoming a professional speaker.

"But Dave... you are a professional speaker. How did you make that happen?"

It was a long road to where I am now. I worked hard at everything I did, advancing in my career as a mortgage broker to own my own multi-state mortgage company. That allowed me to devote a lot of my time and attention to my Kiwanis involvement, including being a state advisor for Circle K. It was there that I practiced and honed my speaking skills and abilities, learning what worked and what did not. I always hoped that some break would come through that would lead me into professional speaking since I did not know any other way.

The break came, eventually. I started attending National Speakers Association meetings where I learned a lot and got motivation to go further. I put up a website, working with one of my former student leaders. (She is still my web designer and I am her longest running client.) I told people that I was a professional speaker, even though I had not been paid yet.

Then it happened. One of my CKI district board members was serving as secretary of her student government. She talked to her advisor about having me lead a goal setting session for their executive board. I did and they paid me an honorarium of a whopping $75. I was on my way!

I continued to make progress. Someone recommended I look for programs that other people or organizations had whereby I could present their material and get paid for it. Right about that time, Kiwanis International was starting a weekend leadership retreat program for high school students called Key Leader. They were going to be doing 30-40 of these events per year and needed facilitators to present the material. And it was going to be a paid opportunity! So, I applied and even though I did not have much professional experience as a presenter, I had presented workshops and trainings for all three of the Kiwanis Family international organizations. They took a chance on me.

It was so great to have someone believe in me and take a chance on me so early in my career. A few days after I got the news, I received a letter from the program manager at Kiwanis International with the contracts, tax forms, and paperwork that I needed to complete. It was so exciting!

As I looked at the letter, I noticed that the advisory committee was listed along the bottom of the stationery. I saw names, occupations, and where they lived. I recognized many of them. The first was a man I knew and under his name it read "High School Educator, Ohio". I recognized the second name, too, a good friend of mine. Under her name it read, "Manager of Training and Development, Illinois." I didn't know the third person across, but I definitely knew the person listed fourth. Under his name it read, "Professor of Leadership, Texas."

Yup.

Twenty years after that guy wrote me the letter that ripped my heart out, I was hired to lead a program he helped create. I never gave up and my victory came, with a little bit of a sweetener!

You will achieve victories too, if you never give up. That is the perseverance of a serving leader.

One of the ways to build your confidence is to flood your mind with positivity. Much of the input into our brains on a daily basis is negative. And we put a lot of it there ourselves. We tell ourselves we are not good enough, not pretty enough, too fat, or too thin. Sometimes we tell ourselves over and over that we are tired. If you say all day, "I'm tired. I'm tired. Oh, I am so tired." What are you going to be? Right!

Instead infuse your brain with positive affirmations.

Affirmations are statements that you tell yourself where you claim victory over what you have now or what you will have in the future. When I set my sights on being the Circle K International President, I wrote in a notebook every day, "I am the President of Circle K International" over and over. I filled a couple of notebooks with that while I was moving up the ladder towards my goal. And I made it happen.

When I embarked upon becoming a professional speaker, I

wrote down no less than 25 affirmations, such as:

- "I am a successful professional speaker."

- "Building Leaders Through Service™ is a powerful, popular, and tremendous program"

- "I am a winner and I see myself achieving my goals."

I wrote personal affirmations, such as "I am a great father," "I am a super husband," and "I am the best District Administrator in the history of Circle K International." These affirmations motivated me to pursue my goals and dreams, even the ones I had yet to get started on. I still say these to this day, including the District Administrator one, even though I retired from that position more than fifteen years ago! I do it to remind me of something great that I accomplished and of which I am proud.

I even had some affirmations that I said for a while and dropped because they were not part of who I wanted to be. The biggest one was, "I am an awesome mortgage broker." I really didn't want to be a mortgage broker any longer, so I chose to stop affirming that. You may revise and update your affirmations as often as you want.

On a piece of paper, write down as many affirmations as you can. State them positively and as if they exist now. For example, "I am a college graduate" rather than "I will be a college graduate." Use this as your guide as you write your affirmations. Say them to yourself daily. I suggest you say them six times per day in the beginning. This will help you to memorize them and make them a part of who you are. Soon you will be believing those affirmations and they will lead you to accomplish things that are important to you.

Leaders use goals to set direction

Serving leaders know where they are going and how they will get there. A key quality under the banner of recognition is to have clearly defined goals. The problem is most people do not know how to set goals and then achieve them.

What do you suppose is the number one day of the year to set goals? January 1? The night before?

And when do you think most people give up on those goals? January 2nd? The night of January 1st?

Does the giving up sound something like, "I jogged a half a mile today... I need cake!"?

Yes! That's because the goals that are set in the deep, dark hours of New Year's Eve or on New Year's Day are missing something: a system for achieving them.

I have a program that provides an easy-to-use framework called the Goal Pyramid System℠ or GPS for short. Step-by-step you, it helps you define what's needed to achieve your goals.

The most important thing is to have a reason for the goals, an overriding vision or dream you want to achieve. Usually they are crazy things like "I am going to lose 70 pounds in a week by jogging 12 miles a day." Really? First of all, if you make it on day one, you won't be able to move for a week. How does someone think they can go from the couch to doing extreme workouts the next day? Plus, where is the dream, the reason for making this effort? What is going to keep our hero motivated to keep jogging and losing weight?

It is called the Dream and it is a vital part of the pyramid.

Dreams can be big, large, abstract visions or very focused blueprints for a single project or activity. Dreams need to be written in such a way as to motivate continual action and progress towards their realization. I used this exact approach to launch my career as a professional speaker. I had been telling people for four or five years that I was a professional speaker, to affirm that in my mind, until I realized I had not done anything to make it happen!

I sat down and decided on a dream that would motivate me to start and continue in my pursuit of this objective:

> "My dream is to make my career as a professional speaker and to glorify God through the use of my skills, talents, and abilities."

"Whoa, that's a pretty spiritual dream. Does mine need to be like that?"

No. It can be, certainly. Mine is because this is part of a spiritual journey for me and how I plan to live the rest of my life. Do I overtly express my faith and preach during my programs? No, but many students come up to me and ask about my faith because they can see it in the way I present. So, I am achieving my dream.

What about our hero above? The one who wants to lose all that weight fast? Perhaps a good dream for him would be, "To get into great physical condition." Ok, now that is a motivating reason to do the work he will need to do to get where he wants to be.

Take a piece of paper and write down all the visions you have for yourself. They can be related to school, career, family, an avocation, or a bucket list item like climbing the Seven Peaks (the highest point on every continent).

Next, pick one of your dreams to flesh out. Craft a statement that will be motivating to you. This will be your Dream Statement and will be at the top of your pyramid. You can use mine above as an example. Another example is the dream I had when I was appointed Georgia Circle K District Administrator: "To be the best district in all of Circle K International and to be the best District Administrator in the history of the organization." Even though that was a volunteer role, I wanted to achieve certain things while I was in the position.

Goal Setting Pyramid

On another piece of paper, draw a pyramid and write your dream statement at the top. This will become a visual representation that will make your journey real.

The journey will have several stepping-stones. These are your goals. These are the things you will have to accomplish in order to reach your dream. You will probably have several goals to help you achieve your dream. Write them down on your paper, brainstorming the things you will need to achieve. Some may be short-term; some may be long- term.

Goals do have some rules to them. A well-known acronym for goals is **S.M.A.R.T.** The letters stand for **S**pecific, **M**easurable, **A**ttainable, **R**ealistic, and either **T**imetable or **T**ruthful. Let's take a look at each of these:

1. **Specific:** Making your goals specific is vital to your success in achieving them. To say, "I want to lose 70 pounds" is great. To say, "I will lose 70 pounds through diet and exercise" is better.

2. **Measurable:** For a goal to be successful, you need a way to measure it. Otherwise, how will you know if you have made it? "I will lose weight" is not measurable. "I will lose 70 pounds" is.

3. **Attainable:** If a goal is truly not within your reach, you will not pursue it. Trying to lose 70 pounds in a week is not attainable, but to set a goal of losing that much weight in six months could be.

4. **Realistic:** This goes hand-in-hand with the concept of attainability. Losing 70 pounds in a week is not realistic, but the other part is the running 12 miles a day. If you have not run in a long time, it is not realistic to think you can run that far and you are setting yourself up for failure.

5. **Timetable:** Setting a deadline creates a sense of urgency for your goals. I never did anything about pursuing a career as a professional speaker until I put deadlines on the goals to make it happen. Our weight-loss guy set a deadline originally of a week, but that is not realistic. Losing 70 pounds in six months and writing out that date forces you to start NOW! The deadline also keeps you focused and moving forward.

6. **Truthful**: The silent "T" of the acronym makes you look deep inside of yourself to make sure you know you will pursue the goal, that the steps to your dream are real, and you will make the effort necessary to get to the top of the pyramid.

The plans on the pyramid are the things you will need to do to make the goal happen. Some may be daily things. Plans also need to fit the S.M.A.R.T. acronym. Some plans for our weight-loss guy could be:

1. To exercise daily, walking two miles, three times per week and lifting weights four days per week
2. Reduce my calorie intake to 1500 per day by the end of next week
3. Document my exercise and food intake in a journal daily starting immediately
4. Get a mentor to keep me on track with my plans and goals by the first of next month

Do you see how much more possible the accomplishment of this weight-loss dream becomes when you are deliberate and intentional about it?

Discussion/Reflection Questions

1. Do you have examples of times when someone has tried to get you to compromise on your values? When? What did you do?

2. Do you consider yourself to be a confident person? How confident are you in your leadership abilities? Do you have people in your life who encourage you and build you up? If so, who? If not, where could you find people like that?

3. Have you experienced discouragement in the pursuit of a dream or a goal that you really wanted to make happen? What was it and what did you do to overcome the discouragement to be successful?

4. What is the first dream that you plan to pursue now that you know how to systematically pursue it with goals and plans?

Chapter Six

Responsible Stewardship

Responsible stewardship is about what you do with what you have been given. That can be talents, abilities, opportunities, resources, money, material items, etc. It can also be a leadership role that has been bestowed upon you, formally or informally. You may be responsible for members, employees, or customers and how you treat that responsibility will determine the kind of leader you are.

There seems to be a dynamic today causing people to say, "It's not my fault."

"It's not my fault that I can't pay my bills."

"It's not my fault that I have a job that I hate."

"It's not my fault that _____ (fill in your own blank)."

That is not what serving leaders do.

Leaders accept responsibility
&
Leaders express genuine generosity

Serving leaders accept responsibility for themselves and those that they lead. A true leader makes decisions, not excuses. Authentic leaders know that sometimes things are not going to go their way, that circumstances may push things off course. As previously discussed, this is where integrity comes into play. True leaders admit their mistakes and work to correct them.

The idea of authenticity seems to be getting diluted in our social media, "sell your brand" world: who people think you are is more important than who you really are. Accept responsibility for who you are and how you lead, and you will find things work out as they should. Being famous for being an influencer on Instagram is not leadership, getting things done is.

If serving leaders are to accept responsibility for what they have been given, then they are responsible for how they distribute and share the resources over which they have charge. You are not some benevolent despot gifting the peasants with your crumbs. You are a leader who must express genuine generosity in the giving of your time, money, efforts, and leadership.

Jesus shares a parable about those coming to the temple to give their gifts and how the wealthy make a big deal and show about doing so (Luke 20:45-21:4). Their reward is that people will look at them and think highly of them for giving so much. Their generosity is through false motives. He continues the parable by sharing how a poor widow came forward and quietly gave a couple of small coins, probably akin to a couple of pennies today. Yet, Jesus praises her because she gave all that she had not to gain acclaim or favor with others but because she felt it was her responsibility to do so.

Do you have a "look at me" attitude in your leadership? If so, people will see it and they will question your motives and why you are involved as a leader. As I wrote earlier, "If you're asking, 'what's in it for me?'", then you are asking the wrong question."

Leaders have a vision

You bring together authenticity, genuineness, and a sincere desire to put others first by having foresight and a vision for who you are and how you will live your life.

If you are involved on campus, think about how you want things to look at the end of your year as a leader of a club or organization. What direction do you hope the group takes? What would you like to have accomplished? What kind of legacy will live on beyond you? How do you do this? By using visualization to create actualization.

See yourself in possession of the things that you wish to have, focus on them, and work towards them. We discussed in the section on affirmations the need to fill your mind with positive images and statements. This step requires you to take this positivity and channel it towards a vision that you want to achieve.

Here is a way to begin creating a vision for yourself:

> Find a quiet place and close your eyes.
>
> Picture where you see yourself three months from now in school, work, activities, in your club or organization, and in your life.
>
> Give yourself some time, anywhere from 20 seconds to a minute.
>
> Then open your eyes and write down what you saw, the ideas you had, and the things you want to make happen.
>
> Repeat this replacing three months with six months, then one year, two years, five years, and 20 years from now.

Write down your vision of these periods in your life.

Make notes on how you are going to move towards those visions.

I did this as part of my process of creating affirmations and my goal pyramid. It helped to coalesce the thoughts and ideas I had for how I was going to become a professional speaker.

Take this process and apply it to your club or organization, programming board, and/or student government. Have your members envision where they see things in a month, two, three… shortening the timeframe to cover this year. Ask everyone to share the ideas, thoughts, and visions they had. This is brainstorming, so there are no bad ideas!

You can also use this same process to examine the various aspects of your organization, for example:

- How do you see our membership?
- What kinds of service projects do you see us doing?
- What new initiatives will we have this year?

And so forth. Write it all down! Then put a plan together to work on the most viable, doable, and exciting of ideas.

This is how you get to where you want to go and leave the kind of legacy that you want others to follow.

Service to others is something that we have modeled for my daughter, Amanda, and our daughter, Katie. We would take both to Kiwanis events, meetings, and projects early on. Katie started going shortly after she was born and went with us to our weekly meetings until she was in pre-K. Many of our members remarked that she had better attendance than they did – which was true!

I recall a project called Soles for Souls our church hosted when Katie was in elementary school. The object was to collect new and gently used shoes for the homeless. Katie made up flyers and gave them to each of our neighbors and also a couple of businesses in the area. She collected 55 pairs of shoes – the second most in the whole church! Katie continued serving her school and church and has considered serving others professionally through her career.

Amanda also got the service bug early. We began taking her with us to conferences and activities after Dia and I got married. She saw service modeled in a way that took hold with her. When Amanda was seven, she and her friends started the Secret Service Club. They would go out at recess to clean up the playground and other areas of the school. They didn't want anyone to know what they were doing, hence the need for keeping it a secret.

Alas, seven-year-olds are not very stealthy and their altruism was soon discovered. The principal was so impressed that she had a video made of their work and it was shown to everyone in the school. Amanda also continued her service involvement into her adult life.

I am very proud of my daughters and pleased with the legacy that carries on with them.

Another legacy that I want to leave is to involve and engage as many students as I can in meaningful service projects that have an impact on others. I do that in big and small ways at conferences, as part of my programs, through my social media posts, and by setting an example by having a strong, lifetime commitment to service.

Leaders have a strong
lifetime commitment to service

I have seen the value of a strong lifetime commitment in so many people. I once spoke at the U.S. Coast Guard Academy in New London, CT. I did a program for the cadets on a Saturday morning and afterwards one of the cadets offered to take me on a tour of the campus.

Tory was a Second Class Cadet, which meant she was a junior in typical, collegiate parlance. She took me all over the campus. They have a great museum with nautical artifacts going back to the 1700s. They have several monuments that she also showed me.

What was really impressive was the Administration Building. In the middle of the building there is a wooden ship's wheel, with a little deck around it. This is a tribute to the fact that the campus is also a working Coast Guard base. Above the wheel on a circular skylight was the honor code, "Who Lives Here, Reveres Honor, Honors Duty."

This was all amazing. Equally amazing was something I saw Tory doing as we went around the base. She was wearing her dress white uniform, as were all the cadets during my program. As we went around the campus she would reach down and pick up trash. Gum and fast-food wrappers, paper, and even a coffee cup with a mixture of coffee, mud, and sticks in it. She put all of these in her pocket – of her dress white uniform!

When she stuck the coffee cup in her pocket I asked, "Tory, is this something you are expected to do? Is it part of the honor code?"

Her response was, "No. I have always done this. I figure that if I pick up one piece of trash every day then there will be 365 less pieces of trash in the world."

Wow, what a great attitude and commitment to have! A couple of years later, I ran into her advisor at a conference who told me that Tory had graduated. She served her required two-year commitment in the Coast Guard and had re-upped for a second tour. That is a person that I am proud to have serving our country!

What is your commitment? Maybe you have some ways you are already serving. Continue those! Perhaps some new ideas have come to you while reading this book. Even if you have not already been serving – get started!

There are many service activities that I enjoy, but I have two major commitments. The first is reading to the kindergarteners I told you about near the beginning of the book. I still go at least once monthly during the school year and we have a great time reading Dr. Seuss books, the adventures of Raggedy Ann and Andy, and more.

I start out the school year by teaching the students a greeting that I learned from a school in Idaho. Think about doing a fist bump with someone and then pulling back with your hand wide open. That is known as doing the "rock" and then "exploding" it. The students in Idaho taught me to say "potato" on the fist bump and then "fries" when opening your hand.

The kindergarteners love it! Every morning their teacher lets them greet each other with either a hug, a high five, or a potato-fries.

The kids remember it as they get older, too. When I am at the school, I sometimes see some of the older kids in the hallways and they get so excited. "Mr. Kelly, Mr. Kelly! You used to read to me!" And then they offer up their fist for potato-fries.

I love that and hope they remember the times when someone cared enough to come read to them.

I have another service commitment is very important to me, too. Do you have a father, uncle, grandfather, friend, teacher, or advisor over the age of 40 in your life that you care about? Tell him to get his P.S.A. tested – it could save his life. P.S.A. stands for Prostate Specific Antigen. It is a simple blood test for prostate cancer which, if caught early, is highly treatable and survivable. As I said, the test could save their life – it did mine!

I am a survivor of prostate cancer. It was caught early, treated with surgery, and there is virtually no chance of it recurring. So, please, share this with a man that you love.

What is your commitment? Some of them can be easy to do, things you can do on your own. Or you may need to involve other people in your commitment and bring other resources into play. Whatever it is, do it! Serve and make a difference in the lives of others.

Post your commitment on my Facebook page for this book and my serving leadership activities: **www.facebook.com/BuildingLeadersThroughService**.

I look forward to hearing about it and everything you are doing as you grow as a serving leader.

Discussion/Reflection Questions

1. When have you accepted responsibility in a formal leadership role? What about in an informal leadership role? What did you do and what was the outcome? What did you learn from accepting responsibility?

2. Have you ever done something for another person or given to a cause because you knew you were going to be recognized for doing so? Did you get the recognition you expected or was there some other result?

3. What kind of legacy do you hope to leave:
   … with your club or organization?
   … on your campus?
   … for your family?
   … to the world?

4. What do you need to do to begin working on the leadership commitment that you made above? Will you need to involve other people? Can you start working on it today?

Conclusion

Thank you for taking this journey with me into serving leadership. My hope is that you will take these ideas and develop the qualities of serving leaders in your life.

You may want to think about this as the **Anatomy of a Serving Leader**:

- **Ears of a serving leader:** listening, conflict resolution
- **Eyes of a serving leader:** vision, visualizations, affirmations, values
- **Feet of a serving leader:** goals – they take you to where you are going
- **Heart of a serving leader:** willingness to take risks, builder of other people and communities, exhibits compassion, leads with integrity, puts others above self, awareness of dreams, goals, and desires of others
- **Hands of a serving leader:** Leaving a legacy, strong lifetime commitment

What comes next? I would love to come to your campus, school, company, organization, church, ministry, etc. to bring this material and these concepts to life. I have versions of this program that I can present as a 30-minute keynote, on up to three hours of highly interactive events.

You can learn more about how to book me for your next event on my website at **www.DaveGonzoKelly.com**. Go to the programs tab and either click on the Keynotes tab and then the program "True Student Leadership" or the Serving Leadership and Civic Engagement tab for several workshop topics to help students get more involved in service.

You can also like my Building Leaders Through Service page on Facebook and follow the activities, events, and service ideas that I post there.
www.facebook.com/BuildingLeadersThroughService

Follow my regular Facebook page at
www.facebook.com/AmericasStudentLeadershipTrainer

I regularly post One Minute Leadership Update videos on my Instagram account **www.instagram.com/gonzospeaks/**

You can also find me on Twitter: **@DaveGonzoKelly**

Lastly, get involved in serving. Either join a club or organization that performs service or start your own! Begin a movement or advocacy that makes a difference. There are many avenues to serve and I am available to you by email anytime at **DaveKelly@GonzoSpeaks.com** if you need help, ideas, or resources.

Best wishes to you for your vision and journey as a serving leader!

"We can change the world.
By serving.
One life at a time."

Dave Kelly

Bonus Chapter:

Planning and Conducting
Service Projects and Fundraisers

It really is important to know how to do the things you have been asked to do. So, this chapter is a how-to of planning and conducting service projects and fundraising activities. This is based on a session I lead that itself is based on a handout my wife created which details a step-by-step process for you to follow. She is a professional event planner and there are things that she thinks about that I do not!

I am about to share 17 steps with you for planning and conducting service projects and fundraisers. There are 4 specific steps to start for each of these two areas and then steps 5 through 17 will be the same regardless of the type of activity that you are planning. By the way, these steps are great to use for planning any type of event, conference, party, etc.

Let's start with **service projects**:

1. **Identify an area of concern that you are interested in serving.** Know who it is that you want to serve and benefit from your efforts. This will help you determine how to best serve that concern and what types of projects will work to accomplish your goals. Some typical areas of concern are children, the elderly, homeless and hungry people, special needs individuals, military service people and/or veterans, environmental, animals, and people with disabilities.

2. **Conduct a needs analysis and survey.** Contact at least three agencies or groups who work with the area of

concern that you want to serve. Ask what they perceive to be the biggest issues and needs faced in this area. Find out how to contribute to improving the situation.

It is tempting to think we have all the answers. It is tempting to believe that there is no possible way the project or activity that we have in mind could not be beneficial. That is not true. I recall a time that my Kiwanis club was trying to come up with some new ways to serve a shelter for homeless men with addictions. We had been providing meals once per month and wanted to do more.

We decided to do a canned food drive in the office building where we met. I called the director of the shelter to ask what kinds of things they needed and the best way to deliver them. It was a good thing that I did because he told me that they did not have a need for canned food donations. They had filled their meal schedule with groups, like ours, that would either come on site and prepare meals for their clients or deliver premade meals from an off-site location. They even had some hotels and restaurants that would provide a meal free of charge as a donation. Food was not a problem for them.

They did have other needs, though. In order to stay in the facility, the men would have to work. Since all of them were homeless before entering the shelter, many did not have clean, presentable clothing for job applications and interviews. They asked us to donate dress shirts, pants, khakis, ties, suit coats, socks, and shoes that their residents could wear to job interviews.

Another need was for suitable reading material to help the men keep occupied while they were in the shelter. There was only one TV and one computer for 40 men. So, whoever got to them first got to use them. We were asked to donate magazines, books, and other materials.

So, we conducted a drive asking for gently used business attire and publications that did not emphasize alcohol, gambling, or other such activities. We had a huge response and did several drives for the shelter. Many members continue to donate clothing and other items. When the agency opened a shelter for women, we conducted a similar drive. We were better able to serve these needs because, fortunately, I called before acting.

3. **Based on your needs survey, decide what kind of project you want to do.** In addition to donation drives, other ideas include marathon events, competitions, arts and crafts, clean-up programs, construction, pet therapy, reading, assembly projects, and more, including combinations of these.

4. **Why should this project be held?** Knowing why you are doing your project is as important as knowing what your project is going to be. You must be able to explain the purpose and benefits to your members, volunteers, and donors. That helps in gaining their buy-in and participation and will go a long way to making your project a success.

Now, on to **fundraisers**. Some of the above concepts will also apply here.

1. **What do you want to raise money for?** Is it for an on-going cause like health awareness, disease research, meals, etc., or a sudden need such as those caused by natural disasters and weather events? Will you be buying something like supplies or building materials or donating

the money to an agency who will put the cash to use and/or distribute the proceeds?

2. **How much do you want to raise?** Have a goal as a target for your group to rally around and donors to get excited about. It can be helpful to tie fundraising efforts to a specific result. For example, in the 1990s, Kiwanis International teamed with UNICEF to work to eliminate Iodine Deficiency Disorders worldwide. It had been determined that a nickel's worth of iodine, over a lifetime, was enough to prevent diseases such as goiter and mental retardation that could be cause by the deficiency. Part of the campaign was promoting every dollar as 20 lives saved. It was very effective and powerful. Moreover, it gave the organization a fundraising goal based on the number of affected people worldwide.

   It is important to emphasize that any money you raise from the public must be spent on the project you have advertised. You cannot say you are raising money to build a playground, for example, and then turn around and use the cash to send delegates to a conference. If your intent is to raise money for the purposes of your club or organization, then that must be clearly conveyed to potential contributors. Also check school policies on fundraising both on and off campus.

3. **What kind of fundraiser do you want to hold?** There are tons of ideas for activities that you can do to raise money and I will be sharing about 80 of them at the end of this chapter!

4. **Why should this project be held?** As with the service projects, knowing why will help energize your volunteers and donors.

Numbers 5 through 17 will be applicable to both **service projects and fundraisers**.

5. **When do you want to hold it?** Think about it from a seasonal perspective: fall, winter, spring, or summer. Then consider the best month in that season for your project. Then, what day of the week works best. Some activities may be themed around a holiday or other celebration, so the time of year may be dictated by that.

   I suggest physically getting out a calendar and looking at the dates you want. Consider things like holidays and school breaks, sports schedules, social events like homecoming or prom, competitions for band and cheerleading, and annual activities. For students, exam times can also be a prime consideration.

   I recall one year that our state executive board was looking at dates for the fall retreat and happened to select a day that is a very sacred religious holiday. Fortunately, a few members of the faith were on the board and pointed it out. That allowed us to change our date.

   Other dynamics can come into play. In most college and university towns Thursday is the social night to go out. That may not be a good time for you to plan a project or fundraiser. Sports is a high priority at many schools, so Fridays for high schools and Saturdays during football season may be times to avoid. Or they may be prime times. Friends of mine who were advisors of a service club at a major university with a strong football tradition found that fundraisers before the games worked great. Apparently, people who are tailgating are willing to give their money away!

Along with choosing the best date(s), think about the best times to do projects. Early in the day? At night? During free/no class periods? How long do you want to be engaged in the project? A couple of hours? All day? Or do you leave it open-ended "until we finish"?

6. **Where do you want to hold it?** Have a primary location along with a couple of back-ups in case your first choice is not available. If you are going to hold it on campus, then there will probably be an official process to reserve a table, a room, a building, or a space. If you want to do it in the community you will probably need to reserve the space, even in a public place like a park, and you might need to obtain a permit for the event.

   Consider also if your site will be accessible to everyone. Not all buildings are accessible to people with disabilities, or the access may be a distance from your actual activity. Some places like parks and beaches could be challenging for people with mobility concerns such as crutches or wheelchairs. Many historic buildings and sites are exempt from the Americans with Disabilities Act and may not have ramps and/or elevators.

   Make sure the site of the project is safe. If there is going to be construction or weather could affect where you are holding your project, then you may want to look at some other options.

7. **Determine the specific goals for the event.** What are you trying to accomplish? Is it to raise a certain dollar amount? Get x number of participants? Assemble so many toiletry packets or make enough doggie tug toys for every animal in the local shelter? These are the typical types of goals that groups have for fundraisers and service projects. But what other goals might you have?

Maybe you are looking to recruit new members for your club or organization. You could be seeking to raise awareness of your cause and/or the activities that you undertake. You might set a goal for service hours performed. Think about all the possible goals that your project could have and include those in your definition of success of the event.

8. **Conduct a S.W.O.T. Analysis.** This is an exercise that you do before the project in which you look at your event from different angles. S.W.O.T is an acronym that stands for:

Strengths: What are the strengths that our members and the organization bring to this project. What types of talents, abilities, and resources do we have that we can use to full advantage to make our event a success? Are there some built-in advantages that we can use, such as affinity groups or agencies that can assist us with the project? Is there common knowledge or a pressing need that provide a marketing and PR advantage/ Do you have a network that can provide materials free or inexpensively? Consider everything that you have going for you. Those are your strengths.

Weaknesses: You can ask the same questions above, only from the perspective of weaknesses or areas that you are lacking in. Do we have enough members to complete this project? Does the campus or community have enough awareness of the issue we are working to help with? What resources, talents, and abilities are we missing? Is someone else already addressing this concern? Is there another major event that is going to affect our participation? Look at all the factors that you are lacking in or are against you. Those are your weaknesses.

Opportunities: What are the opportunities that you have for your service project or fundraiser other than meeting a specific goal? Membership recruitment? Partnering with other clubs or organizations? Involvement of faculty, staff, alumni, and the community at large? The chance to get the word out about what you do? Are there awards that you might receive or could apply for after the completion of the project? Could career connections be made? Consider all the possibilities and those are your opportunities.

Threats: What threats are there to a successful project? Weather? Traffic? Access to the venue? What happens if an accident happens at the entrance to the park, restaurant, etc.? Terrorism? Wide-spread illness? Other events like sports, concerts, testing, and others that could syphon off participation. Members not showing up on time or at all? Everything that could prevent you from conducting your project successfully is a threat.

As you go through each of these areas, catalog your answers and assign people to be responsible for fully using areas of strength and opportunity and others to fill-in the gaps in areas of weakness or threat.

9. **What's your budget for this project?** How much money do you need to spend? Develop a budget of expected income (registration fees, sponsorships, advertising, in-kind donations, etc.) and all expenditures (office supplies, postage, copies, printing, signage, goody bags, food & beverage, permits, thank you gifts/volunteer party, etc.). Will you charge a registration/attendee fee? Who will be paying for your expenses? Will you have sponsors? How will you secure any monies received prior to being deposited?

Regarding fundraisers, any money spent on the project can be reimbursed from the proceeds of the project. Keep receipts so that you can document those expenses.

10. **Timeline your project from start to finish and list the necessary tasks that it will take to plan it.** Assign specific deadlines to the tasks. This is important because some things related to your project may have several components. For example, t-shirts do not just show up on the day of an event. They must be designed, then proofed, then printed, shipped or picked up, etc.

The sample timeline that follows is for fundraisers that are event oriented. Product sales fundraisers will have a different timeline but must have a definite start and end-date. Make sure you also decide how the funds that are raised will be secured before, during and after the event, before they are deposited and/or donated.

Date/Deadline	Task	Person Responsible
12 weeks before	Kick-off meeting with core group of volunteers	Project Coordinator (PC)
11 weeks before	Begin recruiting additional volunteers	PC & Core Volunteers
10 weeks before	Have committee chairs in place	PC
10 weeks before	Review project requirements, begin acquiring and assembling resources	PC & designated volunteers
9 weeks before	Volunteers kick-off meeting/party	All
8 weeks before	Stuff, address & mail sponsorship mailing	Sponsorship Committee
6 weeks before	Review project requirements; continue acquiring and assembling resources	PC & designated volunteers
2 weeks before	Send out press release	PR Committee
1 week before	Review project needs and requirements; finalize materials acquisition	PC & designated volunteers
1 day before	Review checklists one more time; run last minute errands	PC & designated volunteers
TODAY!	EVENT!	All
1 week after	Post-project evaluation	All
1 week after	Volunteer Thank-you Meeting/Party	All
2 weeks after	Final report completed	PC

11. **Who's going to help you?** Create specific job descriptions with as much detail as possible for each position as necessary. Include elements from your timeline (#10).

- The *Volunteer Coordinator* is responsible for recruiting additional volunteers for the project.
- The *Public Relations Chair* is responsible for promoting this project to the public as warranted. They write a press release and distribute it to the appropriate media.
- The *Sponsorship Coordinator* spearheads efforts to obtain sponsorships and donations for the project.
- The *Financial Coordinator* on the day of the event collects all monies, paperwork, runs credit cards, etc. This is not the overall chair or anyone who has another responsibility at the event. This person's sole responsibility is to secure the money, card payments, forms, etc. Do not ask them to help with anything else – that is how bank bags, cash drawers, and documents get misplaced. I have seen it happen!

12. **Conduct the project and a safe professional manner.** This may seem obvious, but it is important to emphasize this point. Even in situations appearing to have no safety issues, neglect or loss of focus could cause injury or other damage.

   This can also extend to the type of clothing required. I have been on some projects where participants must wear closed toe footwear for safety. This can also be a comfort issue if the area is wet or susceptible to getting wet or muddy.

13. **Host a debriefing session immediately following the project** or within a few days to discuss what went well and

what could be improved if the project were to be done again.

I like to go through the entire timeline of the project, from start to finish, including planning, registration, the execution of the project itself, clean-up, etc. One of my ground rules is that if there was something that happened which was an aberration or not likely to happen again, then note it but do not dwell on it. For example, if there was a traffic accident or situation that kept people from making it to the project or getting into the venue. Maybe a key person had a family emergency or illness. You can note it, but there is also probably little you can do in these situations.

Focus on areas for improvement and things that went well. Work on the former and repeat the latter!

14. **Thank your service project volunteers.** Do this with stickers, public recognition, certificates of appreciation, small gifts, handwritten notes, framed team photographs from the project, etc. It is important for people to know they are appreciated and their efforts made a difference in the success of the project or event.

15. **Did you succeed in meeting your goals?** Revisit the goals you set in #7, either during the debriefing session or at an after-event meeting of the planning committee. Consider if some of the goals may need to be assigned for follow-up. For example, if you set a goal to recruit members from the participants, then there should be some effort to contact those people afterwards to invite them to join.

16. **How would you improve this project for the future?** Look at what was done and how and see if there could be some ways to do those things better. Also think about expansion

of the event to impact other people or get more involvement. Things like giveaways, refreshments, and prizes might make the next project more fun and solicit greater participation.

17. **Document the pertinent details of this project for future reference.** This includes contact information of agencies, vendors, suppliers, volunteers, and anyone else that was a part of the project. Do not make the next committee reinvent the wheel by having to do the leg work again. My Kiwanis Club has a par 3 golf tournament every year as a fundraiser. Our committee chair has a binder with the contact info and contract of the golf course we have been using for over 20 years, the caterers that have provided food, the company that makes the hole sponsor signs, etc. This makes it very easy to pass the information down to a new chair and allows for delegation of responsibilities.

Fundraising Project Ideas

_____-A-Thon (walk, jog, hike, read, swim, bike, dance, weight-loss, etc.) All-night movies/cartoons
Apple Bobbing
Art Show
Arts & Crafts Show
Auto Show
Bake sale
Band Party
Barbeque
Basketball Dribbling Contest
Beard Growing Contest
Birthday party
Blind Date Drawing
Book Sales and Exchange
Bowling Tournament
Breakfast & Cartoons Party
Bubble Blowing Contest
Can Recycling
Candy/Flower-grams
Car Demolition
Car Wash
Carnival
Casino Night
Co-ed Softball Tournament
Coin Drive
Concession stand sales
Cookbook sales
Cooking Contest
Dating Game
Donkey Basketball
Dorm Olympics
Dorm/Hall Decorating Contest
Doughnuts & Coffee Sales
Duck Duck Goose Tournament
Dunk Tank
Easter Egg Hunt
Egg Pitching Contest
Face Painting
Fashion Show
Food Eating Contest (watermelon, pie, wings, pancakes, hamburgers, etc.)
Frisbee Contest
Fun-walk/run
Garage sale
Glamour Photographs
Golf/bowling/mini-golf tournament
Hairiest Legs Contest
House-sitting Services
Kiss-A-Mascot
Kite Flying Contest
Marshmallow Roast
Massage
Monopoly Tournament
Mr. Campus Pageant
Pancake breakfast or spaghetti dinner
Pet Parade/Pageant
PJs & Cartoons Party
Poetry Reading/Contest
Powder Puff Football
Pumpkin Carving Contest
Quiz Bowl
Raffle
Sadie Hawkins Dance
Scavenger Hunt
Seed Spitting
Selling product (candy bars, magazines, cookie dough, pizza, doughnuts, scratch cards, candles, coffee, coupon books, wrapping paper, etc.)
Service Auction
Silent/live auction
Sports Tournament
Student-For-Hire (hired for a day with an hourly fee to rake leaves, babysit, mow lawns, or perform other tasks)
Tupperware
VIP Breakfast in Bed
Volkswagen Pushes
Weight Loss Contest

Author Page

Dave Kelly is a professional speaker, trainer, author, and coach. He has spoken and trained professionally hundreds of times during his career for colleges, universities, companies, civic groups, and associations. He loves being a serving leader and shares that passion as often as he can. He is a long-time member of Kiwanis International, a civic community service focused organization.

Dave is a favorite speaker for college and university students. He is an Associate Member of the Association for the Promotion of the Campus Activities and founded and coordinates their community service initiative, *APCA Serves!* He was twice named as the APCA Campus Speaker of the Year, for 2019 and 2022. He is an Associate of the Canadian Organization of Campus Activities, an American Student Government Association Associate Member, and a member of the American Institute of Parliamentarians.

Dave is also the author of *"Gonzo's Little Book of Motivation"* and *"The Sermon on the Mount: The Greatest Motivational Speech Ever"*, and *Building Leaders Through Service: The Qualities of Visionary Leaders [Community Leader Edition]*.

Made in the USA
Columbia, SC
12 August 2023

21462682R00074